DATE DUE

5-11-88			
5-18-88			

Biographies

Paul Laurence Dunbar

A Poet to Remember

by Patricia C. McKissack

CHILDRENS PRESS ™
CHICAGO

ACKNOWLEDGMENTS

Paul Laurence Dunbar's poetry quoted in this book comes from *The Complete Poems of Paul Laurence Dunbar*, by Paul Laurence Dunbar. Published by Dodd, Mead & Company, Inc., New York, New York, copyright © 1913.
Reprinted with permission.

PICTURE ACKNOWLEDGMENTS

Ohio Historical Society—2, 8, 62, 67, 68, 69
The Bettman Archive, Inc.—63 (2 photos), 64, 65
United Press International—66
Cover illustration by Len W. Meents

921
DUN
c. 1
11/87
9.75
4-8

Library of Congress Cataloging in Publication Data

McKissack, Patricia, 1944-
   Paul Laurence Dunbar, a poet to remember.

   Bibliography: p.
   Includes index.
   Summary: A biography of the turn-of-the-century black poet and novelist whose works were among the first to give an honest presentation of black life.
   1. Dunbar, Paul Laurence, 1872-1906—Biography—Juvenile literature. 2. Poets, American—19th century—Biography—Juvenile literature. [1. Dunbar, Paul Laurence, 1872-1906. 2. Poets, American. 3. Afro-Americans—Biography] I. Title.
PS1557.M39   1984   811'.4 [B] [92]   84-7625
ISBN 0-516-03209-7

DEDICATION

To my Mother
Erma Petway Carwell
Thanks for reading to me

Table of Contents

Introduction   9

Chapter 1
    Little Brown Baby   12

Chapter 2
    School Days   17

Chapter 3
    The Philodramians   26

Chapter 4
    Paul, the Elevator Operator   37

Chapter 5
    Poetry in Plantation Talk   47

Chapter 6
    Really Published!   54

Chapter 7
    Jump Back, Honey, Jump Back   70

Chapter 8
    Alice   77

Chapter 9
　A Friend in Need　　　　　　　　　　84

Chapter 10
　Movin' On Up　　　　　　　　　　94

Chapter 11
　A Season of Sorrows　　　　　　　105

Chapter 12
　Lay Me Down Beneaf De Willers...　115

Time Line　　　　　　　　　　　122

Index　　　　　　　　　　　124

INTRODUCTION

Dayton, Ohio, 1872

Many of the black people who settled in Ohio after the Civil War were former slaves. "Sittin' out" was an old custom they had brought from the plantation days. During the long summer months—at a time when there were no air conditioners or electric fans—people sat on their porches or gathered in their yards to cool off and enjoy each other's company.

On the evening of June 27, 1872, those who were sittin' out on Howard Street, in the city of Dayton, paused when they heard the cry of a newborn child coming from the back bedroom of the Dunbar house. Matilda's baby had been born. The neighbors acknowledged the birth by exchanging smiles, winks, handshakes, and even wistful sighs. Then they picked up their conversation where they had stopped.

Inside the Dunbar house, however, the newest family member was greeted with great joy and anticipation. Matilda pressed the tiny infant to her heart and kissed him. This baby was special; he was her first child born in freedom. She had no doubt that *this* baby could grow up to be anything he wanted, including president of the United States. He was a free man—born free! That's what made anything—everything—possible.

"But first things first," thought Matilda. The baby had to have a proper name—an impressive-sounding name that would one day match his successful station in life. Matilda didn't see just a little baby in her arms. Her son was to be a great man, and all great people had grand names. No more ordinary names for any of Matilda's children.

Joshua Dunbar paced outside the "birthing room." Finally he was permitted to go inside. It was a very warm June evening and beads of perspiration glistened on his forehead. The first thing he did was pull back the sheet and look at the little brown baby boy snuggled against his mother.

Joshua smiled; then his smile broadened into a full grin; at last he threw back his head and laughed the laugh of a proud and happy father. "Some day he'll be a great man and do you honor," Joshua told Matilda. His wife nodded her agreement.

"His name should be Paul," Joshua said wiping away a happy tear. The light went out in Matilda's eyes. Her smile faded. She wasn't pleased with her husband's choice of names. Too often Matilda had heard the master of the plantation give his slaves names without meaning. What was the meaning of Paul?

Joshua explained that he was naming their baby after the Apostle Paul, who had been a teacher, preacher, and writer. "Paul was a great man," said Joshua, "and our son will be great too." Again Matilda nodded her agreement.

But her mind had been set on another name. Laurence. She had heard the name in a poem that the mistress of the plantation had read to her years before. Matilda, the slave girl, had saved that beautiful name. When the time came, Matilda, the free woman, could give it to her baby born in freedom. "When I am free," she used to say, "I can name my babies whatever I want, and I won't have to ask permission from nobody." That time had finally come. Matilda was a free woman, but—

"Laurence can be his middle name," she suggested with hope. Paul Laurence Dunbar. Now it was Joshua's turn to nod his agreement. Then he smiled. Matilda smiled back. They had reached a happy compromise.

So it was, then, that when the honeysuckle vines bloomed in 1872, the Dunbars named their son. In the simple act of naming their child, Matilda and Joshua believed they had somehow guaranteed his future greatness. Paul Laurence Dunbar did get a start toward success from two loving parents who believed in the American dream—that anything is possible for a free man.

Chapter 1

LITTLE BROWN BABY

"Paul Laurence Dunbar. That's a mighty high-soundin' name," whispered the Howard Street neighbors, " 'specially for just a lil' ol' biddy baby just one step away from slavery."

Matilda heard them, but she was too busy to worry about their back-fence gossiping. Besides the neighbors' tongues had been wagging about her since she had come to Dayton after President Lincoln had signed the Emancipation Proclamation.

Matilda had come from Kentucky with her two small sons, William and Robert Murphy. Her husband, Willis Murphy, had joined the liberating Union Army, sending Matilda and the boys to live in Dayton until the war ended.

Once in Ohio, Matilda had begun taking advantage of the privileges of freedom. The neighbors' mouths had gaped when she decided to go to night school. Learning to read and write was important to Matilda. After six months she had learned enough to read Bible passages at church and to count her money and keep her finances straight. Learning had been worth the sacrifice.

The war had ended. Willis Murphy never came to Ohio, so they had concluded that he was dead.

In 1871 Matilda had married Joshua Dunbar, a man twenty years older than she. Once again, the neighbors had started their idle chatter. Now Matilda had a new son to take care of; that didn't leave time for her to worry about what the neighbors said or thought about her choice of names.

No baby could have been more loved than Paul Laurence Dunbar. He was a sickly child during the first years of his life, struggling to stay alive. His congested lungs made it almost impossible for him to breathe normally. The child was constantly coughing, wheezing, and gasping for breath. Many times during his first year, it seemed that little Paul would not live through the night. But when morning came, his bright eyes would sparkle and his lips would curl into a happy smile. Then, Ma and Pa knew that their baby had— for the time being—scored a victory over death. But, death didn't leave the house. He crouched in a corner and waited.

It was Matilda's good care that gave Paul his chance to live. The family was poor. There just wasn't enough money to buy the needed medicines or to get Paul the professional medical care he needed. But Ma knew some home remedies she had learned from the herb doctors on the plantation. The homemade brews and salves seemed to help the child breathe better, but he still needed a doctor's care.

Joshua looked for steady work everywhere, but he had no luck. Even though he was an honorably discharged veteran who knew how to read and write, he was still not able to find a job.

Like Matilda, Joshua had an interesting background. And he didn't mind telling people about it, especially his son. When Paul was just a toddler, Pa would call to him, "Come here my little brown baby and sit on your Pa's knee—." Then Pa would begin telling his story, about how he had risked his life to learn reading and writing or about his run for freedom, with the help of a network of people called the Underground Railroad. Paul was just a little boy, but his eyes widened when his Pa told how he had found his way across the Ohio River to freedom and then had gone on to Canada and worked as a plasterer until the Civil War started.

Pa loved to tell Paul how he had joined the Fifty-Fifth Division, under Colonel Norwood Penrose Hallowell, and how he had achieved the rank of sergeant. Pa was proud of his achievements, but they didn't help him now. He needed a job. He hated the idea of his wife supporting the family. Even his stepsons, Rob and Will, did neighborhood chores to help with expenses.

Paul was only two years old when his little sister, Elizabeth, was born. He sat beside the baby's cradle while Ma ironed. Elizabeth was a sick baby, too. As there was no money, there were no doctors and no medicines. Even Ma's home remedies couldn't help. Within a few short months the little girl died. After baby Elizabeth died, Ma turned her full attention to Paul. She was determined that he would live.

Matilda took in washing and ironing for pennies a day. Her days began early and ended late, but she was always cheerful. When she worried, it was not in front of her children. But Joshua despaired. His spirit was crushed, and he began to drink to escape the harsh realities. The alcohol turned his disposition sour and his words bitter.

At first Joshua was quarrelsome; then he began to stay away from home. He tried to stay away as often and as long as he could so he wouldn't have to face the boys. His "job hunting" began early in the morning and didn't end until the family was asleep and he was sure they wouldn't see him stumble up the front steps. They saw him; so did the nosy neighbors.

"Po' Matilda. Chile, she got troubles on her han's. A drinkin' man is a terrible bother on the soul," said the neighbors.

The Dunbars' arguments grew worse. To ease the tension, Ma told the boys stories. Sometimes when Pa was home early and in a good mood, he told stories too. Ma's stories were lighthearted and centered around plantation life. As with any good storyteller, she added a little bit here and took away a little bit there to make the story more lively. When Ma talked about slavery times, she never spoke out of bitterness. But Pa's stories were about battles or were full of the pain and the suffering of slavery. Paul enjoyed Ma's stories more. It was these tales that became the basis of Dunbar's lifework.

One day, when Paul was not quite five years old, his parents had their final argument. Afterwards, Pa gathered his belongings in an old carpetbag and moved out of the house on Howard Street.

"Po' Matilda," whispered the neighbors. "Now she got to raise them young'uns all by herself."

At first Paul missed his father, but things were a lot more pleasant around the house. Will and Rob thought so too; Joshua had been particularly hard on them. Pa moved to the Soldiers' Retirement Home, where Paul visited him regularly. Matilda and Joshua were divorced, but young Paul was always sure of one thing—his mother and his father loved him very much. Being surrounded by so much love made him a loving child.

As soon as he was old enough, Ma taught her son to write his name. The proud mother looked down at the little boy's first attempts, and she couldn't help but smile. "Paul Laurence Dunbar. Now that's a mighty nice name to me," she said. "Sounds just like a preacher."

Chapter 2

SCHOOL DAYS

"You can write your name already?" Paul's first grade teacher was surprised.

Paul smiled. "My Ma taught me how," he said proudly.

Earlier that morning Matilda had told her son, "You're free to learn as much as you want, child. You were born free and don't you forget it."

Six-year-old Paul had promised he wouldn't forget, but he would have promised anything as long as he could go to school. His brothers, Will and Rob, had been going for several years; now it was his time to carry books and do homework. Paul remembered later how grown-up he had felt walking between his older brothers. "You won't be so happy about school when the newness wears off," teased Rob.

Ma had tucked Paul's white shirt into his blue pants. She had starched and ironed them especially for his first day of school. The finishing touch came when she handed him a slate and pencils. Little Paul had no idea how many hours his mother had worked extra to earn the few cents needed to buy his school clothes and supplies. But no matter how much it cost, Matilda was determined that her sons were going to get as much education as they wanted.

At that time, public education was free but not mandatory, so many families chose not to send their children to school. They needed the extra money the children brought in as workers. When Pa had left, Rob and Will had offered to quit school to help out with the household expenses, but Ma wouldn't hear of it. "Go to school. Go to school," she had said, over and over.

But none of that mattered to Paul on that first day of his first-grade year. He would later recall that Fifth District School was just what he had imagined it would be. It smelled like a school should smell. It looked like a school should look.

Paul's teacher was surprised when he wrote his name. She was also surprised when he rattled off his ABCs and then recited his numbers from 1 to 20. That was quite an accomplishment for a first grader in the nineteenth century. Formal education usually didn't begin until the child went to school. Matilda truly did give her son a head start by teaching him at home.

It was in the first grade that Paul discovered words and began a love affair with books and reading that would last a lifetime. Words that rhymed fascinated the youngster, and he created a rhyming game. How many words could be rhymed? "Be and see, high and my, go and so—what rhymes with orange?"

Paul played his special word game many times when he

should have been listening. One day when the teacher was showing the class an important math concept, Paul turned to the back of his spelling book and wrote a four-line poem. It was the first poem he ever wrote and the first of many Fs he would get in math.

It wasn't the way Rob had said. Paul's "school fever" didn't wear off. He loved school and rarely missed a day. And, except for math, he got good grades. His first two years of school were spent at Fifth District. Then the family's financial situation worsened, and they had to move.

Leaving the house on Howard Street was like leaving a part of the family behind. There was so much history in that old house. Paul's great-grandmother and grandmother had lived there. Ma had told him the story many times, so he knew every detail, starting with the abolitionist named Samuel Steele.

Mr. Steele bought Ma's grandmother in Kentucky and brought her to Dayton, Ohio. He freed Aunt Becca, as she was called, and found her the house on Howard Street. Finally he helped her find a job doing laundry. When word of Aunt Becca's good fortune reached the slave quarters back in Kentucky, Matilda made up her mind that she, too, would live as a free woman—one day.

For Matilda's mother, Liza, that day of freedom came unexpectedly. She grew too old and weak to work in the fields. Her master decided it was cheaper to free the old woman than to feed her. Liza was freed to die of starvation or exposure, but she didn't die. She lived. With the help of the Steele family, Liza found Aunt Becca in Dayton. She also found a job, and the two women supported themselves in the house on Howard Street until they died.

It was very hard for Matilda to give up the old home. It wasn't easy for the boys either. But Ma's cheerful attitude was infectious, and the boys soon accepted the move.

In third grade Paul attended Third District School. Then, again the family had to move. Paul began fourth grade at Tenth District.

At Tenth, Paul met many new friends, among them a boy named Robert (Bud) Burns. Bud was an orphan who earned his room and meals by "hiring out." He did work for a family in exchange for food and a place to sleep. Although Bud was a year younger than Paul, they became best friends, a friendship that was to last a lifetime.

More than anything, Bud enjoyed coming to Paul's house after school. Matilda always had delicious things to eat and wonderful stories to tell. Bud always managed to stay long enough for dinner, but Matilda didn't mind. "I've put your name in the pot," she would say. Bud knew that meant that she had prepared enough for him and he wasn't imposing.

After a meal of hot chitlins, wild greens, and corn pone, the boys always begged for a story. One of Ma's stories was as good as her gingerbread—well, almost.

It wasn't that Matilda's stories were better than anybody else's, it was just the way she told them. She had taught herself to speak standard English and wanted Paul to use "proper" English too, but when she got involved in telling a good tale, her language slipped into the smooth rhythmic "plantation talk" known as slave dialect. Her voice became a musical instrument, and her words were like the notes of a beautiful song.

"Tell us about when you were a girl," Paul begged. It was one of his favorites. Ma would begin by telling the boys that she belonged to the Glass family of Kentucky. But all her life she had been sent from plantation to plantation to work for hire. (Bud understood that well.) "I missed my mama somethin' awful. But after a while I got so I could do for myself pretty good."

Then Ma would plunge headlong into a lighthearted yarn about a stingy lady or a stubborn mule, a celebration or a festival. By the time she would finish, she and the boys would be laughing so hard tears would fill their eyes. Then there were other times when the tears in Ma's eyes were not from laughter. Sometimes in the middle of a tale, she would stop and her eyes would turn misty. Only she knew what she was thinking, but Paul knew that she was remembering a bad experience maybe, like Pa. Ma wouldn't talk about it much. When they asked her, she would just say, "Slavery was a terrible thing." Ma wouldn't say much more than that.

21

"Why study on it?" she would say. "It's over. Let it be."

"Tell us about when you almost went to Africa," Paul often pleaded.

Matilda was always ready to oblige. She would begin with her marriage to Willis Murphy and Rob's birth. "I was forced to leave my husband and go where I was sent. That was the worse part of slavery—not having a say over your own life. It was wicked, inhuman—" Fearful that her baby might be sold away from her, Matilda became desperate and planned to run away. She heard about a Back to Africa Movement. She wasn't sure where Africa was or how she would get there, but it was away from slavery. "I was on my way to Africa, but before I could get signed up, President Lincoln signed the Emancipation Proclamation."

Matilda told how she and the other slaves had danced in the big house kitchen for joy. "And that's how come you are a Dayton boy instead of an African boy," Ma said.

Paul laughed. "If you had gone to Africa, you would never have met Pa, and I wouldn't have been born."

"Well, I'm glad I didn't get to Africa, 'cause I wouldn't have missed being your mama for anything in the world."

All through grade school, Paul and Ma remained very close. But Paul also loved to visit his father at the Soldier's Home. Joshua Dunbar was not a happy man. The system had failed him, and he warned Paul that the system would fail him also. At the time Paul didn't know what his father

22

had meant. When Paul was not quite twelve years old, Joshua Dunbar died. His son mourned for him.

Rob and Will quit school before graduating. They got jobs to help Ma with expenses. But no matter how hard times were, Matilda wouldn't discuss Paul's quitting school. She tried not to let her worry show, but by now Paul was sensitive to his mother's moods. Her songs gave him the clues. "Steal Away" was a song that meant Ma had a tough decision to make or that times were hard for her. "Swing Low, Sweet Chariot" was sung when times were good. But, when Ma was especially happy or excited, she would belt out, "When I Get to Heaven."

More and more, Paul noticed that Ma had been singing "Steal Away." He knew why.

The family's financial situation was as bad as it could get. Somehow, Paul felt, he had to do something. Rob and Will had been lamplighters, but now they were working at one of the downtown hotels. Their old jobs were open. Paul and Bud decided to apply for the jobs of lamplighters.

"The job won't interfere with my studies." Paul promised Ma.

"But you're so little," Ma argued. Paul was small for his age. His spindly legs looked like toothpicks, and he looked much younger than he was.

"He's tougher than you think," Bud said. "He can beat us at about any game we play, even though he's smaller."

Ma knew when she was beaten. She agreed, with reservations about schoolwork. The next day Paul and Bud became lamplighters for the city of Dayton.

For one year, the boys met the crew at dusk. From the stables downtown they fanned out, each boy going to his route. Every evening Paul began the ritual of lighting the street lamps. First he positioned his ladder. Then he climbed up, turned on the gas, and touched the torch to the jet. Once down on the ground, he would move to the next lamp and the next until he had his whole block lighted.

Paul often remembered this time before dark. It remained a special time for him all his life. Dusk was a time when shadows changed the shapes of things and the dim light altered reality. At twilight a tree can easily become a giant with outstretched arms—especially for a boy who was to become a poet.

Paul used this time to compose little songs and create funny characters in his head. When he got home, he often wrote his ideas in a notebook—another habit he kept all of his life.

Ma really didn't need to worry. Paul's grades didn't suffer because of the job. He was a very good student in every subject except math. For some reason, whenever the teacher taught math, he just couldn't keep his mind from wandering. "I'll do better in math when I go to Intermediate next year."

"My, my," Ma said. "Things are changing fast." Paul knew that Ma was thinking about his going to Intermediate. Not many of his friends from Tenth got the chance to go any further than elementary school. But he was going.

Other things were changing too. By the end of the year, Dayton no longer had gas streetlights. The city converted to electric lights. Paul Laurence Dunbar no longer had a job. That meant he might not get to continue in school. Late in the night, Paul heard Ma singing "Steal Away."

Chapter 3

THE PHILODRAMIANS

"My name is Orville Wright. My brother is Wilbur, and that fellow over there in the glasses is Ezra Kuhns, but everybody calls him Ez."

Paul had made it to Intermediate! Somehow Ma had done it again. Just when Paul had been sure he would have to quit school and get a job like Rob and Will, Ma had found a way. "I worked plenty hard in my life—for other people," she had told Paul. He had protested about how hard she had been working. "It's a pleasure to work for me and mine for a change."

So here he was. Paul extended his hand; Orville Wright accepted it. And with that handshake, a new friendship began. That afternoon Paul and Orville walked home from school together. They would remain good friends for the rest of their lives.

When Paul rushed into the house after that first day, telling Ma what a wonderful day he had had, she simply smiled and nodded her head. Paul couldn't wait to see his friends from Tenth.

Later that evening Bud and another one of Paul's friends named Charlie Higgins, who was also still in Tenth District, stopped by to hear all about Intermediate. Paul's words seemed to stumble over each other when he told them about the football team and the debate club.

"Only college boys get to play football," said Charlie, wide-eyed with amazement.

"I know, I know," said Paul taking a deep breath.

"Are you going to play?" Bud asked.

Paul nodded his head, *yes*. Ma didn't say anything, so he guessed it would be okay. But more than football, Paul was excited about the debate team. "I know I'm going to join that club," he said.

The first semester went by quickly. Paul played on the football team and joined the debate club. He earned the nickname *Deac*, short for *Deacon* Dunbar, because at fourteen his voice was changing to the baritone of his adulthood. He stood at medium height on a very thin frame. His dark eyes sparkled when he was happy, but looked intensely sad and forlorn when he was unhappy. Paul was rarely unhappy. In his early life, those who knew Paul Dunbar knew him as the lad with sparklin' eyes. He usually passed his joy on to others.

Paul's eighth-grade year ended on a high note. One evening he dashed in from school. He was so excited about something he could hardly talk. After taking deep breaths to calm himself, he told Ma what had happened. Now it was her turn to dance around the kitchen, kicking up her heels.

Professor Wilson, the football coach and English teacher, had complimented Paul on a poem entitled, "An Easter Ode," which he had written in class. Professor Wilson didn't hand out compliments lightly.

Ma encouraged Paul to show his poem to the Reverend Butler at the A.M.E. Methodist Church, where the family worshiped. Reverend Butler read the poem and was so impressed that he invited Paul to recite it on Easter Sunday morning before the congregation.

On Easter Sunday, one by one, the little children stood and nervously recited Easter rhymes they had memorized. For each child there came an encouraging "Amen" from the church elders and nods and smiles of approval from family and friends. It didn't matter if a child forgot half the poem or recited it so fast that the whole thing sounded like one word. Easter in the black church was a time of renewing the body, the mind, the emotions, and the soul. The children were encouraged to answer the New Testament call of "Suffer the little children to come unto me. . . ."

For years Paul, too, had given his recitation before the church body, but today was different. At last it was his turn. Paul walked to the podium. In the debate club he had learned how to stand tall and not show nervousness. He knew not to hurry through his selection; he knew how to keep eye contact with his audience; and he knew how to speak clearly and distinctly. After composing himself, he cleared his throat and began: " 'An Easter Ode' by Paul Dunbar

> *To the cold dark grave they go,*
> *Silently and sad and slow,*
> *From the light of happy skies,*
> *And the glance of mortal eyes. . . ."*

When he had finished and taken his seat, the congregation responded with a hearty "Amen, Amen." Matilda patted his hand. Paul knew that Ma was proud; he was proud of himself. It was the first time he had really shared one of his poems with the public. "An Easter Ode" was all his. He had not memorized somebody else's poem; he had written and recited his own work. He felt as good as he ever had in his life.

A few weeks later, on May 17, 1885, Paul joined the A.M.E. Church and Ma put the membership certificate in the family Bible. She was sure now, more than ever, that her son was going to become a preacher. But Paul was certain after his Easter success that he was destined to be a writer. Nothing else would do.

During the summer, the gang of three added a new member, Randolph Tamms, Randy for short. They were a foursome now, and Ma accused them of being "thick as thieves and twice as secretive." The boys laughed, and their laughter filled the Dunbar house with joy and life.

Will and Rob married and moved to different parts of the state, so Ma no longer had the small contributions that had helped to meet expenses. When the fall school term was about to begin, Paul and Ma counted the pennies, nickels, and dimes in the cookie jar to see what their financial situation was. It was worse than they had thought. Ma had taken in every bit of washing and ironing she could manage; Paul had done odd jobs in the neighborhood; but still there wasn't enough money to pay bills and buy food. High school seemed hopeless. Ma told Paul not to worry about it, and she was so convincing that he didn't.

Help came from an unexpected source. Ma's neighbors, who had often criticized her for wanting too much for her son, suggested that she rent out one of her extra bedrooms. In September 1886, Paul entered Central High School as a freshman. Thanks to the roomer, Ma found they would somehow make it. Once again Paul shook his head at Ma's resourcefulness. She had made a way out of no way.

Central High was like Intermediate, except that the classes were harder and there was more homework to be done in a shorter time. Paul was excited when all the freshmen gathered in the auditorium to hear Captain Stivers, the principal. Paul found his friends Orville and Ezra and compared schedules. Paul had one of his friends in every class. He was glad that Orville was in his math class. Orville was glad that Paul was in his English class. Orville couldn't spell. They could help each other.

When Paul told Bud, Charlie, and Randy about Central,

they were happy for him, but they were enjoying themselves at Intermediate. It was everything Paul had told them it would be—and more.

During the second semester, Paul and Ez were invited to join the debate club at Central—quite an honor. Freshmen were rarely extended such an invitation. Paul's voice was growing deeper and deeper; his posture was more erect and his manner more confident. He was so good and took his debates so seriously that he was soon respected by his classmates, upperclassmen, and faculty.

Before the second semester ended, Paul had another success. One of his poems was printed in the school newspaper. What a wonderful year he had! Ma saved everything that had the name Dunbar printed on it.

His English teacher, Mr. Watkins, suggested that Paul try publishing some of his poems in the *Dayton Herald* newspaper. That same evening Paul put together some of his best poems to send to the local newspaper, hoping he would be featured in the poetry section on the last page. But he knew there was only the slimmest chance that he would be accepted. Only established poets appeared in the *Herald*.

"Nothing hurts a try," said Ma. The odds were against him; Paul sent his poetry anyway. And, like most expectant writers, he waited—and waited—and waited. He watched for the postal delivery, waiting for a response. A response of any kind would have been better than the waiting. Nothing came. After a while he decided to forget it. Of course he felt a little let down, but Dunbar poems were still being printed in the school newspaper. For the time being, that was good enough for him.

In Paul's sophomore year at Central, the foursome was back together in and out of school. Bud Burns had hired himself out to Captain Stivers. The principal of Central was happy to have a bright youngster like Bud living with him in exchange for doing yard work. Captain Stivers placed education and study above yard work and encouraged Bud to stay in school, promising to sponsor the boy through his entire education. Paul was so happy for Bud. Maybe Bud's dream of becoming a doctor was not so farfetched after all.

One summer evening Paul, Randy, and Charlie stopped by to pick up Bud. They had been asked to serve as ushers at the Knights of Pythias Hall on Fifth Street, where the West Side Lodge #5 was sponsoring a minstrel show—the first to come to Dayton. They had to help Bud finish his chores so they would be on time.

"What's a minstrel show?" Bud asked. None of the boys knew what to expect. They were in for quite a surprise.

The show, often called "blackface," featured black and white performers who darkened their faces with soot and then outlined their mouths with white makeup. They told jokes and did skits, using a nonsensical language that was supposed to be black dialect. It was not.

The comedy routine was supposed to be a parody of black life. It wasn't either. It showed blacks as lazy, shiftless, irresponsible, tricky, ignorant, and childlike. The minstrel shows did a great deal to establish black stereotypes that lasted well into the twentieth century.

Why did blacks participate in this negative presentation of their race? Poverty. Historically it was a time of great poverty. Some blacks saw performing in a minstrel show as personally degrading, but a way to eat. They did not consider the long-range problems their actions might cause. Often these blacks were northerners who had neither been slaves nor knew anyone who had been a slave. At the time they were not concerned about the historical accuracy of the content of their performances.

The white performers were also using the minstrel show as a meal ticket. They were simply capitalizing on popular demand. Audiences all over the country enjoyed seeing blacks portrayed as buffoons and rascals. When the show was over, the whites washed their faces. The blackness was gone. A black minstrel player also washed his face. The black stayed on, and so did all the negative stereotypes.

Some audiences thought the minstrel show was harmless entertainment. "It's just fun. . . ." But others recognized that it was dangerous and offensive. It was demeaning to black actors. Long after the soot had been removed, the role of the fool was the only one open to black actors. Into the first half of the twentieth century, black actors still would be cast as slow-talking idiots. There were no black heroes in early twentieth-century American drama.

Neither Paul nor his friends were impressed with the minstrel show. In fact, they were convinced that they could give a far better performance. "We can start a real drama club of our own," Paul suggested. His buddies agreed. "I have even thought up the name," he said. "*Philo*, which means 'fond of'; *dramian*, which means 'drama'— Philodramians."

The club met twice a week at Paul's house. Ma always had a big pan of gingerbread fresh from the oven waiting on the table. Paul wrote, directed, and starred in the first Philodramian play, *The Stolen Calf*. The plot was very simple.

A group of boys—much like Paul and his friends—stole a calf and sold it so they could buy tickets to the circus. When the school principal found out, he bought the calf, returned it to the rightful owner, and then bought the boys tickets to the circus. The little thieves were very excited, believing they had gotten away with getting something for nothing. But their principal had other plans. He made the boys do chores in his house and yard to earn the money for the calf— and their tickets. The work was hard and dirty, so the lesson they learned was a good one.

Everybody agreed that the play was a worthy production,

suitable for audiences young and old, so the premiere of *The Stolen Calf* was given at the Baptist Church in Yellow Springs, Ohio. It was so successful that the boys were invited to perform the play at several other churches in the Dayton area. The admission charge, which was very little, was divided—half for the poor box and the other half for the club.

Meanwhile, Paul's friends at Central were doing exciting things too. Orville and Wilbur Wright had started their own newspaper, called the *Midget*. The Wrights had put together a homemade printing press and had set up their barn as a print shop. They took jobs printing handbills to support their newspaper, which was growing in popularity.

Orville told Paul that he wanted to print some of his poems. Paul accepted the invitation, but it wasn't the same as being published by the *Herald*. Orville was Paul's friend; he would print his poems no matter what. But the *Herald*—

"I'm just not a very good poet," Paul said to Ma one evening a few weeks before his sixteenth birthday. After almost eighteen months, he still hadn't heard from the *Herald*.

"Oh, yes, you are," Matilda said. "You are good!"

The *Herald* agreed with Ma. On June 8, 1888, Dayton's leading newspaper printed Paul's poem, "Our Martyred Soldiers." Then on Friday, July 13, 1888, his poem, "On the River," was printed. What a wonderful sixteenth birthday present!

Ma said, "Read it to me again." He began, " 'On the River,'
by Paul Dunbar.

> *The sun is low,*
> *The waters flow,*
> *My boat is dancing to and fro.*
> *The eve is still,*
> *Yet from the hill*
> *The killdeer echoes loud and shrill."*

Ma listened to every word, and no matter how many times
she heard him read the poem, it was new and fresh to her.

It didn't matter to Paul or Ma that he hadn't been paid.
Paul Laurence Dunbar was a real poet. Was there anything
else in the world more important? Paul didn't think so.

Chapter 4

PAUL, THE ELEVATOR OPERATOR

"Yes, I know we have published your poems, but we have a policy. We don't hire colored reporters here at the *Dayton Herald*."

Paul was astonished. He knew he was black. He knew there was prejudice in the world. But he had never been hit so squarely in the face with it. He began to wonder, "If this is what I am to expect, what did Ma work herself half to death for?"

Paul walked outside the *Herald* offices. He was confused and hurt. He couldn't help but remember the last two years. It had been a hard time for him and Ma, but they had seen it through.

In January of his senior year, Paul had caught a cold. It started like a typical winter cold—sneezing, headache, light coughing. Then the infection had settled in his lungs, and within a few days Paul was flat on his back in bed. For weeks Ma had nursed him back to health. He was lucky to be alive.

When Paul had finally been able to go back to school, he had fallen so far behind in his math he was unable to catch up. He remembered Captain Stivers calling him into his office. "I'm sorry, Paul, but you will not be permitted to graduate." The words had hurt. But even knowing that he wouldn't graduate with his class was not as hurtful as now being told he was not good enough to hold a job in a company because he was black.

With Ma's help he had come to accept the setback at school as a temporary one. In the fall of 1890, he had returned to Central to repeat his senior year. It had been easy, because all of his good friends had been with him.

That year, Paul had taken Orville's and Wilbur's idea and had begun publishing the *Tattler*, a newspaper for the black community. The Wrights had printed it for him. Unfortunately, black people were buying bread instead of newspapers, and the *Tattler* had folded after only a few issues. Meanwhile, Paul had become the editor of the school newspaper and president of the debate club. He had been a popular and well-respected student.

Then on June 16, 1891, Paul had graduated, along with thirty-eight other classmates. The *Dayton Herald* had printed: "The beautiful farewell song, composed by Paul Laurence Dunbar, colored member of the class, was sung by the graduating class, closing the exercise."

But now Paul stood on a street corner wondering which way to go. The rejection he had felt inside the *Herald* offices had shaken him. He pulled himself together and went to other places that day. He looked for work in offices, but the response was always the same: "No colored hired." One office manager laughed at Paul, another swore at him, and still another questioned his honesty about being a high-school graduate.

Racial bigotry had not been a problem for him all his school days—well, almost. He recalled his junior year when he had not gone to a picnic. He had known that he would have been accepted by his white friends, but his date would not have been accepted by the girls. At the time he had thought of it as a girl problem, not a race problem.

But the situation was serious. Paul was being denied a job—a way to make a living—because of his skin color. What was he supposed to do? He had been given a wonderful education by his mother—an education many whites weren't fortunate enough to have. Yet he couldn't find a job. Paul fought to keep himself from being furious.

By the end of the first day of job hunting, Paul was willing to accept any job.

Over dinner one night, Paul talked to Ma. "I don't understand," he said. "I was good enough for the *Herald* to publish my poems, but I'm not good enough to be one of their reporters."

Ma just nodded her head. She had a deeper understanding about those things than she was willing to admit just then. Paul was depressed enough. Why depress him more? "Something will come up," she answered cheerfully. "One day those *Herald* people will be glad to publish anything you write. Just you wait and see." Ma believed in her son.

At the time, Paul didn't believe in himself. Yet, the next morning he was out early. By evening he was hardly able to drag his body up the front steps. He was not really physically tired. After being told over and over that there was no work for a colored man, he was completely drained emotionally. His self-esteem had dropped as low as it had ever been, and his mind reeled with conflicting thoughts.

What was happening? Paul talked over the problem with his friends, Bud, Charlie, and Randy. Why were all the doors slamming in black people's faces? They weren't slaves any longer. Why were they being treated differently?

No one had the answers, but they had some ideas. At the end of a long discussion, the group agreed that the solution to the race problem rested with a man known and respected throughout the United States as the black crusader— Frederick Douglass. His had been the strongest voice against slavery, and after emancipation he had taken a prominent position in government.

But the young men from Dayton didn't realize that Douglass's voice was fading. The nation's interest had shifted from slavery to winning the West. The Civil War had split the South and the North. The West became a common ground where old wounds could be mended. Out there a new enemy had been manufactured—the American Indian.

40

Little did Paul and his friends know then that the "black problem" was being turned over to individual states to handle as was "fitting." The southern states and many of the border states were seeing fit to pass unconstitutional laws that would prohibit the rights of black people for well over a hundred years after slavery had been abolished. The laws would not be challenged and overturned by the United States Supreme Court until the 1960s.

Paul did not give up hope, and at last he found a job in the shipping department of the National Cash Register Company, lifting heavy boxes. He was so tired after the first few days that he began to cough. Finally he had to quit.

It was an awful time, but Ma's happy spirit kept him from falling into despair. Then, at the end of the summer, Paul was hired as an elevator operator for four dollars a week. It was a decent salary and the work was not backbreaking; but it was boring, especially for a young man with a sharp mind. Soon, however, Paul learned to use his job for gathering ideas. Some very interesting people came in and out of the Calahan Building, and he made mental notes about how they looked, talked, and walked. At night he recorded his observations and ideas in a notebook. When he needed characters in a poem or story, he pulled out his notebook and developed fictional people based on his notes. That's why Dunbar characters always seem so alive. They really were.

Now being an elevator operator didn't seem so bad after

all. One day a lady stepped on the elevator and smiled. "So you're Paul Laurence Dunbar," she said. "Four, please."

On the way up, Paul learned that the lady was Mrs. Frank Conover, whose husband was a well-known Dayton lawyer with offices on the entire fourth floor of the Calahan Building. Paul acknowledged that he was the same Dunbar whose poems had appeared in the *Herald*. (He didn't mention that the *Herald* had refused to hire him because he was black.) Mrs. Conover called Paul one of Dayton's best young poets. She encouraged him to continue to write. Whenever she was in the building, Mrs. Conover visited with the young elevator operator-poet. In time they developed a friendship that lasted many years.

When Paul wasn't taking a group up or down, he kept his pen and paper near his stool. He filled his spare time reading, particularly the *Century*, and told himself that one day he would be published in that fine literary magazine. Then he would feel comfortable calling himself a poet.

One article in the *Century* affected him deeply. It was about the Jim Crow laws the southern states were passing, laws that separated races in schools, on public transportation, and in hotels, restaurants, and businesses. Paul couldn't understand how this could be happening and why nobody seemed to be able to stop it.

Out of his anger and frustration Paul Dunbar wrote one of his most famous poems, "Ode to Ethiopia." It has become an

American classic. He didn't care if it was ever published; he wrote it for himself. Out of a troubled spirit and compassion for his people and their suffering, the young poet poured out his feelings in simple straightforward language.

O Mother Race! to thee I bring
This pledge of faith unwavering,
  This tribute to thy glory.
I know the pangs which thou didst feel,
When Slavery crushed thee with its heel,
  With thy dear blood all gory.

Sad days were those—ah, sad indeed!
But through the land the fruitful seed
  Of better times was growing.
The plant of freedom upward sprung,
And spread its leaves so fresh and young—
  Its blossoms now are blowing.

The last two stanzas are beautifully simple and reveal the poet's love for and pride in his race.

No other race, or white or black,
When bound as thou wert, to the rack,
  So seldom stooped to grieving;
No other race, when free again,
Forgot the past and proved them men
  So noble in forgiving.

43

Go on and up! Our souls and eyes
Shall follow thy continuous rise;
Our ears shall list thy story
From bards who from thy root shall spring,
And proudly tune their lyres to sing
Of Ethiopia's glory.

Paul Dunbar continued to write and study. He learned that there was a lot of interest in stories set in the West, with outlaws, shoot-outs, lawmen, gamblers, cattle rustlers, and a wild assortment of other villains and heroes. Paul knew very little about the West except for what he had read, but he wrote two stories anyway, "The Tenderfoot" and "Little Billy," which, to his surprise, were taken immediately by Kellogg Syndicate in Chicago. Kellogg handled stories that were carried in newspapers nationwide. Overnight Paul became a nationally read author. Plus, he was paid six dollars for both stories—the first time he had been paid for his writing. That made the sale a double bonus. Still he was a long way from being able to support himself with his writing.

One day, while Paul was sitting on his stool at the Calahan Building waiting for passengers, he saw his former English teacher, Mrs. Helen Truesdell, coming toward him. She was breathless with excitement. Before Paul could do more than greet her, she asked him to give the welcoming address at the Western Writers' Association Convention. Paul was delighted, and accepted on the spot.

Paul decided that instead of giving his presentation in prose, he would use poetry. He worked evenings and during his spare time at work to perfect the rhythm and rhyme of the poem.

Then, on his twentieth birthday, Paul presented his poem to the writers' group. He was unable to enjoy the thunderous applause because he had to hurry back to his job. With only an hour for lunch, he had one minute in which to get back to his station at the Calahan Building elevator. He couldn't afford to lose his job—yet.

The next day Dr. J.N. Matthews and three other members of the writers' group came to see the young elevator operator who could write poetry. They had to ride up and down with Paul so as not to interfere with his work. They asked to read more of the poet's writings and invited him to read some of his material before the group the following evening. "That is, if you don't have a prior engagement."

Paul chuckled to himself. He wanted to kick up his heels and shout for joy, but he calmly accepted the invitation with all the poise and dignity he had learned to project as a member of the debate team.

But Ma didn't care much about poise. When he told her, she danced around the kitchen with uninhibited joy. Her son was working as an elevator boy, but he was also a poet.

45

There, Ma had finally said it. Her son was a poet, if not a preacher. Paul Laurence Dunbar—poet.

Chapter 5

POETRY IN PLANTATION TALK

"Enclosed is a check for $2, payment for your dialect poem, 'Banjo Song.' Signed, the Editor."

Paul shared the short acceptance letter with Ma. All the reading and research he had been doing had been worthwhile. For weeks he had been reading the works of other writers: Eugene Field, author of "Wynken, Blynken, and Nod"; James Russell Lowell; and especially, James Whitcomb Riley, who wrote in Indiana Hoosier dialect. Paul had found Riley's work the most interesting and had studied the Indiana poet's style and content. By analyzing Riley's poems almost line for line, Dunbar believed he had discovered the key to Riley's public appeal—characters.

Riley developed characters with whom his audience could easily identify, whether they were Indiana Hoosiers or Washington statesmen. Paul could see Riley's characters and actually hear them talking. They were never wooden or stiff.

"I can write dialect, too," Paul had said. "I'll use slave dialect." And so he had. The first dialect poem Paul Dunbar wrote was "A Banjo Song," which he sold to the *Chicago News Record*.

Ma couldn't understand how a poem written in "plantation talk" could possibly be of any value. All her life she had been trying to rid herself of slave dialect, and she was particularly proud that Paul spoke standard English flawlessly. He wrote in standard English, too. So why was he using dialect? Ma wasn't so sure she liked it at first, even though the verses were humorous and the people in them were like real people she had known as a child. Since it was Paul who was writing the poems, she finally decided that somehow they must be all right.

Paul, too, had his own misgivings about writing in dialect. The minstrel shows had made fun of plantation talk and the people who spoke it. They had made a mockery of the language, the people, and their customs. Paul was determined that this would never happen in anything he wrote. But it was somewhat difficult to write about something he had not experienced himself. His only real contact with slavery was through his mother and father, and Matilda had done all she could to take the ugliness out of slavery. So the people Paul wrote about tended to be like Ma—happy, pleasant-mannered people, who were doing the best they could.

"A Banjo Song" was not the first piece of literature to use slave dialect. Joel Chandler Harris had written the Uncle Remus stories years before Paul wrote his poems. But Harris had written in prose, using animal characters instead of people. His stories were told by a man named Uncle Remus,

48

a slave. Harris was not careful about the accuracy of the language; his interests were in storytelling, so there are many words and word variations in the Remus stories that are not true to black language patterns.

Other black writers had written in dialect, too, but unsuccessfully. Paul Dunbar was the first black to write poetry in slave dialect with as much sensitivity and love for the language as he had for the people who spoke it. This is what assured his success and earned him the title of black poet laureate.

The characters in Dunbar's poems, like those created by Riley, were real, with feelings and experiences that were common to all people. Beneath the humor was usually a serious tone that revealed the spirit of the people on whom he modeled his characters—people like his Aunt Elizabeth and Ma, who were able to make the most out of a bad situation. Dunbar made it quite clear that behind every smiling face there was not necessarily laughter.

Examine for a moment the character in "A Banjo Song":

'Bout de time dat night is fallin'
  An' my daily wu'k is done,
An' above de shady hilltops
  I kin see de settin' sun;
When de quiet, restful shadders
  Is beginnin' jes' to fall,—

49

Den I take de little banjo
F'om its place upon de wall.

. . . .

An' my wife an' all de othahs,—
Male an' female, small an' big,—
Even up to gray-haired granny,
Seems jes' boun' to do a jig;
'Twell I change de style o' music,
Change de movement an' de time,
An' de ringin' little banjo
Plays an ol' hea't-feelin' hime.

This banjo player is neither a minstrel fool nor an ignorant rascal. He is a human being.

Slave dialect was not just random, incoherent utterances. There was a definite pattern to the speech. For example, most *ing* endings were dropped; *falling* became *fallin'*. The *th* sound was replaced with the *d* and the *f* sounds; *the* became *de* and *with* became *wif*. The *dow* sound became *der*; therefore, *shadow* became *shadder*. The *er* sound became *ah*, changing *mother* to *mothah*.

Parts of words were often dropped; *'bout* was a shortened form of *about*, *'most* was short for *almost*, and *'cept* was another way of saying *except*. Words were spelled as they were pronounced; so *get* became *git*, *your* became *yo'*, and *just* became *jes'*. Sometimes the final *d* sound was dropped from

50

words; thus *sand* became *san'*, *hand* became *han'*, and so on.

Finally, it is important to understand that the slaves very often created words. *Disremember* is an example, as is *gwine*, which means "going."

Slave dialect was not consistent. A Tennessee slave used words differently from the way a Louisiana slave used them. There were as many variations of slave dialect as there were slave states. For this reason, the reader finds that words and pronunciation change from poem to poem.

It was not until much later that Dunbar wrote "Little Brown Baby," which has become an American classic in slave dialect. It is based on the poet's early memories of his father. In the evenings, before Joshua Dunbar became a bitter and sad man, he would call his son to come sit on his knee. Then he would tell Paul the wonderful stories of adventure and escape and sometimes even tease him about the "Boogie Man," who was supposed to live just outside their door.

The love between father and son in the poem crosses racial lines. Fathers of every race have shared this poem with their children, but minority fathers are particularly fond of this Dunbar piece. It presents a black father and son in a loving relationship, something that is rarely shown in American literature. This one poem has helped to destroy the myth that black fathers don't care about their children when in fact, they do; they always have.

Little brown baby wif spa'klin' eyes,
  Come to yo' pappy an' set on his knee.
What you been doin', suh—makin' san' pies?
  Look at dat bib—you's ez du'ty ez me.
Look at dat mouf—dat's merlasses, I bet;
  Come hyeah, Maria, an' wipe off his han's.
Bees gwine to ketch you an' eat you up yit,
  Bein' so sticky an' sweet—goodness lan's!

Little brown baby wif spa'klin' eyes,
  Who's pappy's darlin' an' who's pappy's chile?
Who is it all de day nevah once tries
  Fu' to be cross, er once loses dat smile?
Whah did you git dem teef? My, you's a scamp!
  Whah did dat dimple come f'om in yo' chin?
Pappy do' know you—I b'lieves you's a tramp;
  Mammy, dis hyeah's some ol' straggler got in!

Let's th'ow him outen de do' in de san',
  We do' want stragglers a-layin' 'roun' hyeah;
Let's gin him 'way to de big buggah-man;
  I know he's hidin' erroun' hyeah right neah.
Buggah-man, buggah-man, come in de do',
  Hyeah's a bad boy you kin have fu' to eat.
Mammy an' pappy do' want him no mo',
  Swaller him down f'om his haid to his feet!

Dah, now, I t'ought dat you'd hug me up close.
Go back, ol' buggah, you sha'n't have dis boy.
He ain't no tramp, ner no straggler, of co'se;
He's pappy's pa'dner an' playmate an' joy.
Come to you' pallet now—go to yo' res';
Wisht you could allus know ease an' cleah skies;
Whist you could stay jes' a chile on my breas'—
Little brown baby wif spa'klin' eyes!

Chapter 6

REALLY PUBLISHED!

"I'd like to buy six copies of your book, *Oak and Ivy*, to give as Christmas books," said Mrs. Conover. Paul smiled as he handed his friend six books. In two weeks he had sold enough copies to pay Mr. Blocher the $125 he had invested in the publication of *Oak and Ivy*.

The last few months had gone by so fast, Paul couldn't imagine how it all could have happened, but it had.

It had started with a visit from Orville Wright, who often stopped by the Calahan Building to visit with his old high-school chum and find out what had been happening in his life. Paul had told him about some of his poetry successes, and Orville had shared the news that he and Wilbur had given up the newspaper, *Midget*, and were doing only large printing jobs. But Orville still liked to tinker, and he was tinkering quite a bit lately. "Do you think man will fly?" Orville had asked Paul.

"Sure," Paul had answered. "As sure as I'm going to be a great poet one day, man will fly."

Orville had smiled. "I think so, too," he had said seriously. Then Orville had gone on to suggest that Paul try to get a book of his work published. "Try the United Brethren

Publishing House, and be sure to mention my name. My dad's a bishop now," Orville had said on his way out the door.

Paul hadn't wasted a moment. He had gathered all his poems—some in dialect and some in standard English. He included his favorite—the one he had never shared before, "Ode to Ethiopia." That would definitely be in his book. Half the fun had been selecting his own poems, then arranging them. At last Paul named his book of poems *Oak and Ivy*.

Once he had checked his manuscript, he had taken it to be published. The editor had rejected the manuscript without even a reading. "Sorry, but we just don't sell poetry well. Times are hard and people aren't buying poetry books." The manager, Mr. Blocher, had told Paul they would print his book, if he paid for the first printing. The book foreman had quoted him a price of $125! It might as well have been one million dollars. Paul had turned to leave.

Then Mr. Blocher had called him back. He had agreed to pay the $125 print costs, provided that Paul would repay the money out of his first earnings. The young poet had consented without hesitation.

Two weeks before Christmas, the books had arrived. Paul and Ma opened the box together and examined the first books. The title was stamped on the cover in gold letters, and when they opened the book to the title page it read *Oak and Ivy* by Paul Dunbar; next was the date, 1893. Although the book had been produced in 1892, the printer had played it safe and typeset 1893 in case the books were delivered late. Next came the dedication page. Ma had smiled broadly as she traced the words with her fingers, "To my mother who has ever been my guide, my teacher and inspiration."

Three days after publication, Paul had sold eighty-five copies at one dollar each—and Mr. Blocher had been paid in full two weeks later. Christmas that year was joyful, complete with all the trimmings.

By late January Paul had earned enough for a small down payment on a house at 140 Ziegler Street in Dayton. Although the new house was close to the center of town, there was still room for Ma to raise a few chickens. There was also a yard with beautiful flowering shrubs; a large snowball tree was always Paul's favorite. In February of 1893, Paul and Ma moved in.

After the publication of *Oak and Ivy*, Dunbar's reputation as a poet began to grow. Invitations to speak came regularly, and his performances were so well received that word of him began to spread. Every weekend he was engaged to speak before audiences throughout the Midwest. The pay was very small, usually just travel expenses and sometimes a dinner at the sponsor's house. But book sales were always good after a performance.

Mrs. Conover remained Paul's best customer, often buying five or more copies of his book at a time. "I love giving your books as gifts," she said on her way up to the fourth floor.

"Thank you," said Paul.

"I'm always happy to help Dayton's best poet," she responded. And she was true to her word. Mrs. Conover sent a copy of *Oak and Ivy* to a young lawyer in Toledo, Ohio, named Mr. Charles Thatcher. Thatcher wrote Paul a letter; Paul replied. Then the two of them agreed to meet in Toledo when Paul passed through on his way to Detroit to give a reading. Thatcher was so impressed with the young poet that he invited him to speak at the fashionable West End Club, a literary society in Toledo. Paul accepted.

On his return trip from Detroit, Paul stopped in Toledo. Thatcher met him at the train station and escorted him to the club. Paul knew that he was the second speaker on the program; he had no idea who was first. Since the meeting was about to start when they arrived, Thatcher and Paul took seats near the back of the room. Paul listened attentively as Dr. W.C. Chapman was introduced. His topic was "The Negro in the South."

Paul was very interested in what Dr. Chapman had to say about southern blacks, for he had never traveled in the South himself. He sat forward as Dr. Chapman began his presentation: "The Negro is not educable... the Negro is lazy... the Negro is sly and cunning...."

Paul could not believe what he was hearing! His heart pounded in his throat; his hands became sweaty. What was this man saying? Why was he saying such things? Paul wanted to leave—no, he thought he just wanted the floor to open up and swallow him whole. Somehow he remained seated and poised. He sat as tall and straight as he could. Except for him, there were no blacks in the room, but since he was sitting in the back no one noticed.

At last Dr. Chapman's presentation ended to scattered polite applause.

It was time for the next speaker. The appropriate introductions were made and Paul heard his name called. He stood and walked forward, almost in a trance, but with his head held high. He later confided to friends how he felt. He said it was like carrying the entire black race on his back as he walked up the aisle.

The young poet was angry, but he put those angry thoughts out of his mind. He was hurt, but he tucked those hurt feelings in his back pocket. He had to stay in control. He could fall apart later, he told himself. He was tense until he opened his mouth—then he knew he was ready to accept the challenge. He began speaking with controlled passion. "I shall give you a poem I had not intended to read tonight. It is called, 'Ode to Ethiopia.'"

Chapman was too embarrassed to stay; he slipped out a side door.

Paul read the poem with feelings even he didn't know he had. Then he ended with:

Go on and up! Our souls and eyes
Shall follow thy continuous rise;
  Our ears shall list thy story
From bards who from thy root shall spring,
And proudly tune their lyres to sing
  Of Ethiopia's glory.

The crowd roared its approval. The poet had defended his people well. Charles Thatcher was delighted. Had Thatcher known the content of Chapman's speech? Is that why Paul had been invited? Paul often wondered if his presence at that particular meeting was by accident or design. The two men never discussed it, and he never knew.

Shortly after Paul's return to Dayton, Thatcher wrote him, offering to sponsor Paul's education at Harvard, which would generously include a fifty-dollar-a-month allowance—plus any other expenses! The young elevator operator thought about it, but politely refused—not out of arrogance, but he just preferred to pay for his own education. However, he did follow Thatcher's advice to send a poem to the *Toledo Blade* and *Bee* newspapers.

Soon afterward a copy of the *Bee* arrived with his poem printed in it, with an editorial comment attached. "In Paul Dunbar, the young colored poet who recited before the West End Club, Ohio has a practical genius who will be heard from in the near future. . . . He combines the ease and grace of a Riley with the sentiment and diction of a Longfellow."

After that, the Dayton *Herald* editor took a second look at Paul Dunbar. Policy wouldn't allow Dunbar to work in the office, but there was nothing that said he couldn't do freelance assignments for them. Paul accepted the assignment from the *Herald* and shook his head at the foolishness of their hiring policy.

One day in early spring the *Herald* editor asked Paul if he were going to the Chicago World's Columbian Exposition. Paul had given it some thought. Rob and Will were living in Chicago and had been writing him to come. Jobs were supposed to be plentiful. On the spur of the moment, Paul said, "I've been seriously thinking about going."

"Good," responded the editor. He assigned Paul an article called "Dayton at the Fair." Without a moment's hesitation, Paul gave notice to the Calahan Building manager and caught the next train to Chicago.

Ma was miserable about Paul's leaving, but he promised to send for her when he could.

When Paul arrived in Chicago, he realized that every young man in the country must have had the same idea. The fair was not scheduled to open for another month, but people were everywhere. There wasn't a place that wasn't overflowing with people. And the plentiful jobs? There were a few openings for blacks. Chicago was cold and windy, big and frightening. In his first letter to Ma, Paul tried to sound cheerful, but in his heart he wasn't very happy. "I miss you something awful," he wrote. "Love, your son Paul."

Matilda Dunbar

The Wright brothers,
Wilbur (left) and Orville
(below) went to school
with Paul Dunbar.
Paul and Orville were
good friends throughout
their lives.

The main street of Dayton in the 1890s

Frederick Douglass

A photo of Paul Dunbar taken in 1890.

Paul Dunbar and Alice Moore were married on March 6, 1898.

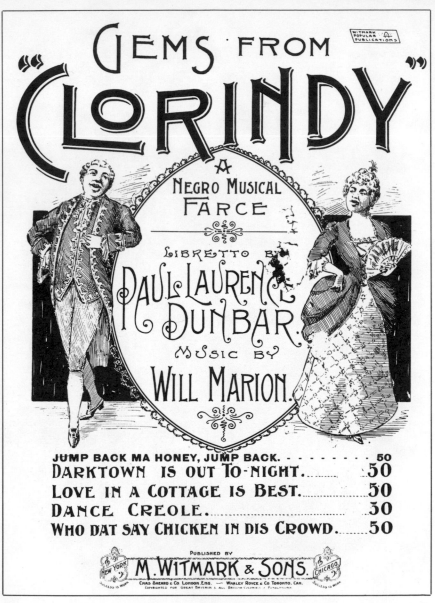

The musical *Clorindy*, with lyrics by Paul Dunbar, was an instant hit when it opened in New York City.

The last house Paul Dunbar lived in was at 219 North Summit Street in Dayton.

Chapter 7

JUMP BACK, HONEY, JUMP BACK

"I'd like you to meet my grandfather, Frederick Douglass," said Joseph Douglass. Paul couldn't believe that he was standing in the presence of Frederick Douglass, leader of the black race in America. All Paul could think about was how glad he was that he had stayed in Chicago, even though it had been so lonely those first two weeks.

When he arrived in Chicago in the spring of 1893, Paul's brothers had been glad to have him, but their quarters were small. There really wasn't a lot of room and absolutely no privacy.

The opening of the Chicago World's Columbian Exposition was to be in May. Paul looked for work, but was not lucky. Then he heard about a job in a downtown restaurant. He applied and was hired. The hours were terrible but the pay was six dollars a week. He rented a room in a boarding house. Paul was now a waiter. But he was still a writer, so his ears were listening for the unusual. He heard it in the restaurant.

There was a swinging door leading from the kitchen to the dining room. Before going through the door with a heavy tray and possibly colliding with someone, the waiters would yell, "Jump back." Then for safe measure they'd repeat the warning, "Honey, jump back." Meanwhile, the kitchen buzzed with the sound of waiters who were busy gossiping about their dates. The cook often sang a song that he made up as he went along.

Paul listened to the rhythms of the warning and the chatter of the waiters. After work one evening, he wrote "A Negro Love Song":

> *Seen my lady home las' night,*
> *Jump back, honey, jump back.*
> *Hel' huh han' an' sque'z it tight,*
> *Jump back, honey, jump back.*
> *Hyeahd huh sigh a little sigh,*
> *Seen a light gleam f'om huh eye,*
> *An' a smile go flittin' by—*
> *Jump back, honey, jump back.*
>
> *Hyeahd de win' blow thoo de pine,*
> *Jump back, honey, jump back.*
> *Mockin'-bird was singin' fine,*
> *Jump back, honey, jump back.*
> *An' my hea't was beatin' so,*
> *When I reached my lady's do',*
> *Dat I could n't ba' to go—*
> *Jump back, honey, jump back.*

Put my ahm aroun' huh wais',
  Jump back, honey, jump back.
Raised huh lips an' took a tase,
  Jump back, honey, jump back.
Love me, honey, love me true?
Love me well ez I love you?
An' she answe'd, " 'Cose I do"—
  Jump back, honey, jump back.

Without a doubt this poem is Dunbar at his best. Who can sit still when they hear the rhythm of this poem? School-children have been skipping rope and chanting this song for many years, "Jump back, honey, jump back!"

James Carrothers, another writer, had told Paul how he might be able to earn a few extra dollars. Chicago news-papers were paying six dollars for good human-interest articles. So, Paul had gone to the fairgrounds in search of a story. It was there that he had met Joseph Douglass, the grandson of Frederick Douglass, who was at the fair in charge of the Haitian exhibit.

Everybody knew who Frederick Douglass was—a leader, orator, writer, and statesman who had been born a slave somewhere in Maryland about 1817. But Joseph told Paul special things about his grandfather when they sat together over a sandwich. Paul learned that Frederick Douglass's father had been white, but that his mother had been a slave.

His maternal grandmother had cared for him until he was sent to Baltimore to work as an errand boy. The boy's new mistress had taught him the ABCs. Using this bit of knowledge, Frederick Douglass had learned to read the word *freedom* and to understand that it was guaranteed in the United States Constitution. "Grandfather did not rest until he escaped to freedom, and he has devoted his life to helping his brothers," Joseph told Paul.

Joseph was proud of his grandfather's accomplishments, and rightfully so. As an abolitionist, Douglass had used his talent for giving stirring speeches to further the cause of black people. He had pleaded time and time again for men of reason and compassion to join him in the struggle to abolish an institution that maimed the spirit of a whole race of people.

When the Civil War ended and black people were free, Douglass became an early supporter of women's right to vote. "Right has no sex," said Frederick Douglass. In 1889 he had been appointed U.S. minister to the Republic of Haiti. It was in this capacity that he had come to the Chicago fair. After listening to Joe, Paul couldn't wait to meet the elder statesman.

When Paul stood before the aging warrior for the first time, he felt awestruck. But as always he managed to pull back his shoulders and maintain his poise. "So you are the young poet I've been hearing so much about," Douglass said.

Paul wanted to say, "Who me?" but he bowed slightly to acknowledge that he was. From then on it was as though they had known each other for years. Paul read Douglass' "Ode to Ethiopia," but not with the defensive passion with which he had responded to Dr. Chapman. This time he read it with the love he felt for this kindly black gentleman who had done so much for his people.

Douglass enjoyed "The Ol' Tunes" and other Dunbar dialect poems. At the end of the visit, Paul hurried home to write Ma. "I gave him a copy of *Oak and Ivy*, although he insisted upon paying for it. 'Well,' he said, 'if you give me this I shall buy others,' so, I expect to sell him two or three anyhow."

By the first of June Paul sent for Ma. When she arrived, she took a room in the same building where Rob and his family lived. She was just in time to learn that Paul had quit his job as a waiter and was working instead as Mr. Douglass's assistant.

Working in the Haiti exhibit gave Paul an opportunity to meet fascinating people, which made up for the cut in salary he had taken. Paul told Ma he would have worked for Frederick Douglass for nothing. She believed he would have, but she was glad he was getting some money.

Some of the young blacks with whom Paul had become acquainted decided that the fair should have a Colored Americans' Day. Friday, August 25, 1893, was set as the date. The celebration began at 2:30 P.M., with almost three thousand people gathered at Festival Hall. A few white teenagers came, expecting to see a minstrel show. But when Frederick Douglass began his speech, "The Race Problem in America," the youngsters began to hoot and jeer. Furious, Douglass put away his prepared speech and, like the old crusader he had once been, took on his foes.

"There is no Negro problem. The problem is whether American people have loyalty enough, honor enough, patriotism enough, to live up to their Constitution. We Negroes love our country. We fought for it. We ask only that we be treated as well as those who fought against it."

The jeering stopped as the old lion roared out these truths!

After Douglass, there were several other speakers, and then Paul Dunbar was introduced. He stood at the podium and read his poem, "Ode to Colored Americans." Ma sat in the front row, as proud as she would ever be. Her son was on stage with Frederick Douglass.

The fair lasted until October 28, 1893. It was closed when Chicago's mayor was killed by a madman. That ended the jobs. Blacks were especially hurt by the layoffs. Whites could find work, but there were few jobs for blacks. The long party ended. The lights were shut off and people went back home. Paul said his good-byes and promised to visit. Two years later Frederick Douglass was dead.

Before they parted, Frederick Douglass gave Paul a copy of his book *Life and Times*, an autobiography that has become an American classic. Inside Douglass wrote a long inscription: "To one of the most promising young men of our time. From Frederick Douglass to a dear young poet friend, Paul Dunbar, one of the sweetest songsters his race has produced and a man of whom I hope great things."

Paul would remember the man who had been his personal friend and an inspiration to millions in a poem entitled simply "Frederick Douglass."

> *A hush is over all the teeming lists,*
>   *And there is pause, a breath-space in the strife;*
> *A spirit brave has passed beyond the mists*
>   *And vapors that obscure the sun of life.*
> *And Ethiopia, with bosom torn,*
> *Laments the passing of her noblest born.*
>
> *She weeps for him a mother's burning tears—*
>   *She loved him with a mother's deepest love.*
> *He was her champion thro' direful years,*
>   *And held her weal all other ends above.*
> *When Bondage held her bleeding in the dust,*
> *He raised her up and whispered, "Hope and Trust."*

Chapter 8

ALICE

"Welcome back to your old job as elevator boy. We missed you around here," said the Calahan Building manager. Paul was happy to have his job back but he was not so happy about being an elevator *boy*. He was twenty-one years old now and feeling a bit uneasy about the direction his life was taking. After rubbing elbows with a man like Frederick Douglass and with the people who had visited the Haitian exhibit, it was difficult for young Dunbar to settle for being an elevator operator; yet he couldn't be too choosy just then. Times were very hard for a lot of people in Dayton. He was lucky to have a job—any job.

After the fair Ma had decided to stay in Chicago with Rob, because his wife Leckie needed help with their new baby. Paul had gone home. The house wasn't the same without Ma. He had looked for other work, but when the bills began to mount, he had had to return to the Calahan Building.

Orville Wright came by one day on one of his regular visits. He had come to tell Paul that the Wrights wouldn't be able to print his handouts any longer because they were closing their print shop. They had opened a bicycle shop. Orville told Paul all about his classmates. Charlie Higgins was a fully ordained minister with his own church; Randy Tamms was studying law at night school; and Bud, who had been working with Dr. Reeves, had finally gone on to medical school at Western Reserve in Cleveland. Sitting beside the elevator, Paul wondered whether he would ever amount to anything.

Times were especially hard. Ma was writing home every week that she wanted to come home in time for Christmas. But he didn't have the money to send for her. What could he do? He applied for a job as a teacher, but was turned down because he didn't have a college degree. He never felt so alone.

The bank was about to foreclose on the house. He had no place to turn. In desperation Paul wrote to his friend, Mr. Thatcher, and explained the situation. Within days the lawyer sent Paul fifty dollars. Paul paid the house note and all outstanding bills and still had money enough to send for Ma.

With Matilda back, the house was home again. Good smells drifted from the kitchen. His clothing was fresh. The bed sheets smelied like cool, clean air.

That Christmas of 1893 he and Ma looked over their year. "This time a year ago," Paul said, "my book had just come out. I wonder what the new year will bring?"

One day, early in 1894, Paul received a letter from *Century* magazine. Paul nervously tore open the envelope. The magazine in which he had been trying to get published since he was sixteen years old had finally accepted not one, but three of his poems. Inside was a letter from the editor: "Three of your poems have been accepted for publication— one of which is my favorite, 'A Negro Love Song.' " Signed R.U. Johnson, the Editor.

Paul slapped his knee and clapped his hands. Then he grabbed Ma around the waist and sang, "Jump back, honey, jump back! Oh! Jump back, honey, jump back!"

After *Century* published his poems in 1894, the name Paul Dunbar was recognized by editors. More of the poems he sent out were accepted; when a piece didn't sell, the editor wrote him a personal note asking for something more specific or giving him an assignment.

Mrs. Conover still had not forgotten Paul. She arranged for him to meet George Cable, a writer whom Paul admired. He was speaking in Dayton. Much to young Dunbar's surprise, Cable knew of him and asked for an autograph.

By summer Paul was again faced with a career decision. He was offered a job as the editor of a black newspaper—the *World* in Indianapolis, Indiana. There was only one problem. The job was not permanent—it was only until the regular editor returned. Paul took the job, believing that it could lead to something better. Also, the experience was invaluable.

Looking through a literary magazine one day, Paul saw a picture of a beautiful woman named Alice Ruth Moore. She was a writer, too! He was quite taken by her beauty and fell in love with her picture. Paul decided to write her a letter.

When she did not answer immediately, Paul decided that she wasn't interested and forgot about the whole silly thing—well, almost. Then one day he received a letter at the boardinghouse where he was staying in Indianapolis. The handwriting was not familiar.

Paul opened the letter and read: "Dear Sir: Your letter was handed to me at a singularly inopportune moment—the house was on fire!"

Paul was hopelessly in love. Alice was beautiful, smart, and had a sense of humor. She went on to explain that although the fire had been small, in her excitement she had forgotten the letter until she found it a few days later on her desk. Afterward they wrote to each other regularly.

Paul went home to Dayton to spend his twenty-second birthday with Ma. After he had used his salary to pay the house note, there wasn't enough left for a party. So he wrote about one and called it "The Party." Long ago, when Paul was a young boy, Ma had told him about such a party:

> *Dey had a gread big pahty down to Tom's de othah*
> > *night;*
> *Was I dah? You bet! I nevah in my life see sich a sight;*
> *All de folks f'om fou' plantations was invited, an' dey*
> > *come,*
> *Dey come troopin' thick ez chillun when dey hyeahs a*
> > *fife an' drum.*

Evahbody dressed deir fines'—Heish yo' mouf an' git
  away,
Ain't seen no sich fancy dressin' sence las' quah'tly
  meetin' day;
Gals all dressed in silks an' satins, not a wrinkle ner
  a crease,
Eyes a-battin', teeth a-shinin', haih breshed back ez
  slick ez grease;

. . . .

Paul described the good food that the guests provided. It was a traditional soul-food menu.

We had wheat bread white ez cotton an' a egg pone jes'
  like gol',
Hog jole, bilin' hot an' steamin' roasted shoat an' ham
  sliced cold—
Look out! What's de mattah wif you? Don't be fallin'
  on de flo';
Ef it's go'n' to 'fect you dat way, I won't tell you nothin'
  mo'.
Dah now—well, we had hot chittlin's—now you's tryin'
  ag'in to fall,
Cain't you stan' to hyeah about it? S'pose you'd been
  an' seed it all;
Seed dem gread big sweet pertaters, layin' by de
  possum's side,

Seed dat coon in all his gravy, reckon den you'd up
and died!

. . . .

Well, we eat and drunk ouah po'tion, 'twell dah was n't
nothin' lef,
An' we felt jes' like new sausage, we was mos' nigh
stuffed to def!

What is a party without dancing? Paul described the fun
everyone had.

Tom, he knowed how we'd be feelin', so he had de
fiddlah 'roun',
An' he made us cleah de cabin fu' to dance dat suppah
down.
Jim, de fiddlah, chuned his fiddle, put some rosum on
his bow,
Set a pine box on de table, mounted it an' let huh go!
He's a fiddlah, now I tell you, an' he made dat fiddle
ring,
'Twell de ol'est an' de lamest had to give deir feet a
fling.
Jigs, cotillions, reels an' breakdowns, cordrills an' a
waltz er two;
Bless yo' soul, dat music winged 'em an' dem people
lak to flew.

*Cripple Joe, de old rheumatic, danced dat flo' f'om
    side to middle,*
*Th'owed away his crutch an' hopped it; what's
    rheumatics 'ginst a fiddle?*
*Eldah Thompson got so tickled dat he lak to los' his
    grace,*
*Had to tek bofe feet an' hol' dem so's to keep 'em in deir
    place.*
*An' de Christuns an' de sinnahs got so mixed up on
    dat flo',*
*Dat I don't see how dey'd pahted ef de trump had
    chanced to blow.*
*Well, we danced dat way an' capahed in de mos'
    redic'lous way,*
*'Twell de roostahs in de bahnyard cleahed deir th'oats
    an' crowed fu' day.*
*Y' ought to been dah, fu' I tell you evahthing was rich
    an' prime,*
*An' dey ain't no use in talkin', we jes' had one
    scrumptious time!*

Ma was laughing so hard she had to gasp for air. "Paul
Dunbar," she sputtered, "you can tell a story as good as me."

The following day Paul returned to his job in Indianapolis.
But when fall came, the editor returned and Paul was
unemployed again. Reluctantly he returned to Dayton.

Chapter 9

A FRIEND IN NEED

"Sorry, Paul, but your job has been taken by a more responsible boy," said the Calahan Building manager.

Paul stood looking at the Calahan Building where he had worked since his high-school graduation. Now, he didn't have a job. Somehow he wasn't worried. In fact, he felt relieved. Being an elevator *boy* was not what he wanted to do all his life. "I can be a full-time writer," he thought. Instead of walking with his head down, he threw back his shoulders, lifted his chin, and walked home whistling.

Mrs. Conover still kept in close touch with Paul; she continued to send *Oak and Ivy* to influential people she knew within literary circles. And, it was through Mrs. Conover that Paul came to know Dr. H.A. Tobey.

Paul had been invited to speak before the Western Writers' Association, which was meeting in Indiana. His topic was to be writing the short story. Unfortunately, Paul didn't have the money to make the trip. He tried borrowing from family and friends, but none of them had money to spare. It was almost certain that he would have to cancel. Then a letter came that would change the poet's life. The letter was postmarked Toledo, but it wasn't from Mr.

Thatcher. When Paul opened the letter, five dollars fell on the floor. The letter had been sent by a Dr. Tobey, and the five dollars had been enclosed to pay for a copy of *Oak and Ivy*.

Paul read the letter as Ma anxiously listened.

> ... I am in a position to give you financial aid if you desire to increase your education or to travel with a view of better qualifying yourself to pour out your poetical songs to the world.

Who was this strange man? Paul wondered. At the time he didn't know that Dr. Tobey was a humanitarian who had the ability to fulfill the promise he made in his letter.

Those who knew Dr. Tobey later reported that his interest in Paul Dunbar began when he received a copy of *Oak and Ivy* from Mrs. Conover, along with a letter praising the elevator boy who was a poet. The young poet's determination to succeed in a field that was usually reserved for the well-educated or the wealthy interested Dr. Tobey. Paul was neither college trained nor wealthy; yet, he had accomplished a great deal on his own.

Investigating Paul's background, Dr. Tobey had learned from Mr. Thatcher and others that Paul had paid back the $125 it had cost to print his book of poems and that he had used his earnings to purchase his mother a home. Thatcher, who also had been impressed with Paul from the start, told

Dr. Tobey that young Dunbar was proud, but not arrogant; poised, but not pompous; dignified, but not pretentious. After hearing all this about Dayton's young poet, Dr. Tobey was impressed. This was a young man of integrity and promise. And Dr. Tobey wanted to help him succeed.

Paul answered Dr. Tobey's letter after he returned from the Western Writers' Conference. He told the doctor that the money had come at the right time for him to make the trip to Indiana. Paul and Dr. Tobey began corresponding. Now Paul had two people to write to every week—Alice and Dr. Tobey.

The romance between Paul and Alice developed through the mails. They grew to care very much for each other, but were afraid to call what they felt for each other love. They had never met. Paul had never seen the sparkle in Alice's eyes nor heard the sound of her laughter. Alice had never seen Paul's proud strut, with head held high, nor heard the mellow tone of his voice. Yet, somehow he knew that he loved her; and from her letters, he knew that she loved him too.

Paul had come to expect letters from Alice and Dr. Tobey and others, but one day he received an unexpected letter. It was from Will Cook, a young playwright whom he had met in Chicago. Cook wrote to say that he had composed music for "A Negro Love Song" and had sold it to Witmark Music Publishers. Will also said he was writing a musical,

Clorindy, the Origin of the Cakewalk, and asked if Paul would agree to write the lyrics. The poet readily accepted the assignment.

Meanwhile, Ma had gone back to Chicago to help Rob and Leckie. She wrote regularly. Alice continued to write, as did Dr. Tobey, but Paul was still lonely. So, in August, when an invitation from Dr. Tobey arrived, Paul immediately accepted. Dr. Tobey, who was the director of the State Mental Hospital, asked Paul to give a reading for the patients. In truth, it was really an opportunity for the two men to meet.

The two men liked each other as soon as they shook hands at the train station. Tobey was tall, medium built, with piercing blue eyes and a dark brown beard. Paul was tall too, but he was very thin and his eyes were as dark as a swamp night. His skin was like black velvet, and the ease with which he spoke the language gave him the confident demeanor usually reserved for royalty.

Dunbar presented his program to the patients at the hospital, and while they didn't always understand what was being said, they enjoyed Paul's animated presentation and clapped in time to the rhythmic poems. The day was wonderful for both patients and poet. After dinner, Dr. Tobey's wife and two lovely daughters were given a private reading that Paul had especially prepared.

Again, Dr. Tobey and Mr. Thatcher offered the poet money to attend Harvard University; again Paul rejected their offer. Still, Dr. Tobey insisted that he be allowed to do something to help. Together he and Thatcher decided that they could advance Paul's career by paying for the printing of a second volume of Dunbar poems.

Paul returned to Dayton and gathered the poems for his second book. He selected some of his writings in dialect and some in standard English. He wrote a number of new poems—mostly love lyrics written for Alice. The second volume of Dunbar poems was called *Majors and Minors*.

Alice liked Paul's standard English poems and told him they were her favorites. To her the "jingles in a broken tongue" were not his most important contributions, and she "awaited the day that he no longer had to include them in his books of poetry."

Paul began to view his dialect poetry differently. At first he had been willing to try any style that would help him get published. He had seen no harm in writing dialect. But now he began to feel that perhaps all the attention he had been getting because of his dialect poetry was not good. It was, to him, a novelty that really had no lasting literary value.

What Paul and Alice and others of his day failed to realize was that his dialect poems were unique, beautiful, rich in ethnic culture, and original. His standard English poems were, at best, imitations of styles already made popular by other—and better—poets.

Majors and Minors was published in 1895. Like *Oak and*

Ivy, Paul's second book was dedicated to his mother. Paul's one disappointment was that the printer had misspelled his middle name, making it *Lawrence* instead of *Laurence*.

On January 15, 1896, Paul sent a copy of *Majors and Minors* to his little niece, Ethel, Rob's daughter. On the inside leaf, he wrote:

> *Brown of hair and brown of eyes,*
> *Growing daily flowerwise.*
> *Like a little flower too,*
> *Gentle sweetness through and through.*
> *Witching with an artless art,*
> *Little Lady Loving Heart.*
>
> *Loving Heart thou art to me,*
> *So I send this book to thee.*
> *Ethel dearest, let it be*
> *Just a tender memory*
> *That shall breathe to you and all*
> *Of your loving Uncle Paul.*

What a wonderful way to inscribe a book! Even as a grown woman, Ethel remembered the joy of receiving that volume from Uncle Paul.

One of the best-remembered poems in *Majors and Minors* is "When Malindy Sings." It is about the mistress of a plantation who tries to sing, but can't. In the poem a slave jokes about Miss Lucy's singing, telling her, and everyone else listening, that Malindy is the singer—and without needing a music book.

G'way an' quit dat noise, Miss Lucy—
　　Put dat music book away;
What's de use to keep on tryin'?
　　Ef you practice twell you're gray,
You cain't sta't no notes a-flyin'
　　Lak de ones dat rants and rings
F'om de kitchen to be big woods
　　When Malindy sings.

. . . .

Ain't you nevah hyeahd Malindy?
　　Blessed soul, tek up de cross!
Look hyeah, ain't you jokin', honey?
　　Well, you don't know whut you los'.
Y' ought to hyeah dat gal a-wa'blin',
　　Robins, la'ks, an' all dem things,
Heish dey moufs an' hides dey faces
　　When Malindy sings.

In the "Majors" section, Paul included "Frederick Douglass" and countless love poems he had written to Alice. Among the other poems in this section is a four-line verse that has been memorized by schoolchildren all over the world for nearly one hundred years.

DAWN

An angel, robed in spotless white,
Bent down and kissed the sleeping Night.
Night woke to blush; the sprite was gone.
Men saw the blush and called it Dawn.

Two other poems in this work deserve special mention. "We Wear the Mask" and "An Ante-Bellum Sermon" are written in two different styles. "We Wear the Mask" is written in standard English; "An Ante-Bellum Sermon," in dialect. But both show the racial awareness growing in the young poet.

One day after *Majors and Minors* had been published, Paul received a note from Dr. Tobey saying: "Get a copy of *Harper's Weekly* and read what William Dean Howells thinks of you." Paul hurried to the newsstand, purchased a copy of *Harper's Weekly*, and read what Howells, the famous literary critic of that day, had to say about him and his writing. Paul knew that if Howells gave him a favorable critique, that could mean instant success.

He nervously found the page and read:

> I hope the reader likes as much as I like the strong, full pulse of the music in all these things. Mr. Dunbar's race is nothing if not lyrical, and he comes by his rhythm honestly.

But what is better, what is finer, what is of larger import in his work is what is conscious and individual in it. He is, so far as I know, the first man of color to study his race objectively, to analyze it to himself and then to represent it in art as he felt it and found it to be; to represent it humorously, yet tenderly, and above all so faithfully that we know the portrait to be undeniable like. A race which had reached this effect in any of its members can no longer be held wholly uncivilized; and intellectually Dunbar makes a stronger claim for the Negro than any Negro had yet done.

Paul was so moved by Mr. Howells's praise that he felt obliged to write him:

July 13, 1896

Dear Mr. Howells:

I have seen your article in *Harper's* and felt its effect. . . . I can tell you nothing about myself because there is nothing to tell. My whole life has been simple, obscure and uneventful. I have written little pieces and sometimes recited them, but it seemed hardly by my volition. . . .

The praise that you have accorded me will be

an incentive to more careful work. My greatest
fear is that you have been more kind to me than
just. . . .

Again thanking you, Mr. Howells, for your
more than kindness. . . .

After Howells's review, Paul became a celebrity. Everywhere he went people shook his hand and introduced him as the famous poet from Dayton. Paul was an accepted writer but he didn't feel very different. At the end of summer, a reception in Paul's honor was held at the home of Dr. Tobey. Ma came from Chicago to be with him there. After shaking hands with the governor of Ohio and the mayor of Toledo, the young poet was excited and a bit overwhelmed by his good fortune. Later, in the quiet of his room, he composed a poem, "The Crisis." It ends with the poem's speaker saying:

> *"Mere human strength may stand ill-fortune's frown;*
> *So I prevailed, for human strength was mine;*
> *But from the killing pow'r of great renown,*
> *Naught may protect me save a strength divine.*
> *Help me, O Lord, in this my trembling cause;*
> *I scorn men's curses, but I dread applause!"*

Paul gave a copy of the poem to Dr. Tobey. It was Dunbar's way of saying thank you and of assuring his patron that he would not let his sudden rise to the top turn his head.

Chapter 10

MOVIN' ON UP

"Paul Dunbar, I am going to get you a deal with one of the largest publishing houses in New York," said Major James B. Pond.

With the help of his sponsors, Paul had hired Pond as his literary agent. Pond was to handle the up-and-coming poet's speaking engagements and contracts for his book publications. There was something about the major that Paul didn't trust, but he couldn't put his finger on it.

Major Pond had handled such noteworthy people as Mark Twain, Henry Ward Beecher (the brother of Harriet Beecher Stowe, author of *Uncle Tom's Cabin*), and Frederick Douglass. When Paul heard that Pond had handled Frederick Douglass, he felt a little more comfortable with the New York fast-talker.

The first thing Pond managed was to convince Paul that he needed to leave Dayton and move to New York, where he could be in the mainstream of things. Dr. Tobey agreed with Pond, and so Paul packed his things. With a new suit purchased for the occasion, he left for the big city.

By the first of August 1896, Paul was settled in New York. The move proved to be a good one. Paul renewed old friendships he had made at the World's Columbian Exposition and through those friends, he met new people, mostly writers, artists, actors, and teachers.

Pond began taking Paul around to major publishing houses. Harper, Appleton, and Dodd, Mead were the largest in that day. These publishers knew of the young black writer and wanted to publish his next work. It was Dodd, Mead who made the best offer—a $400 advance against royalties, 15 percent royalty on the first 10,000 copies, and 17 percent on all sales beyond that. Paul couldn't believe those figures. The advance alone was more money than he had earned in a year as an elevator operator.

Ma was back in Chicago with Rob, and Alice was teaching school in Boston. Alice was so near but still so far away. They continued to write to each other and hope for a chance to meet. Alice's parents were opposed to her having anything to do with a writer, especially a poor one. Also, he was not a college graduate, and Alice was. They felt that it would be a poor choice for their daughter to marry a man with no more visible means of support than his writing skills. Everybody knew that a writer's salary was not secure. What would happen when he was no longer popular? How could he support a wife? A family?

Alice didn't agree with her parents' reasoning. She loved Paul and continued to write to him. But Paul couldn't give Alice's parents answers that would ease their minds, so he held off proposing marriage until his career was more stable.

Dodd, Mead published Paul's third volume of poems, entitled *Lyrics of Lowly Life*. Again Paul dedicated the book to his mother. William Dean Howells had agreed to write the introduction, and the book was an instant success. White readers bought *Lyrics* by the thousands, but among well-educated blacks there was some reserve. While they saw Dunbar as having the potential to be a "real poet," they considered dialect poems to be a kind of novelty with no real lasting literary value. There were even a few blacks who resented Dunbar's dialect poems and accused him of being a "minstrel show poet." This hurt Paul deeply; it was never his intent to represent black people as ignorant or foolish.

William Dean Howells wrote in the introduction of *Lyrics to Lowly Life*:

> I say the event is interesting, but how important it shall be can be determined only by Mr. Dunbar's future performance. I cannot undertake to prophesy concerning this; but if he should do nothing more than he has done, I should feel that he had made the strongest claim for the Negro in English literature that the Negro has yet to make. . . . In more than one piece he has produced a work of art.

Howells praised Dunbar's dialect poems but felt that his standard English poems were not particularly brilliant. Suddenly, Paul had a growing uneasiness. Somehow he felt boxed in by Howells and others who praised his dialect and disregarded his standard English writing. The critic had said his best works were his dialect poems. Was there respectability in writing only dialect? Could a black person write about other things besides the black experience? He wondered.

This marks the beginning of Dunbar's personal discontent. He would never feel comfortable with his dialect writing again. He confided to a friend, James Weldon Johnson, another black poet from Florida, that he was not happy about the turn his writing had taken. He said:

> You know, of course, that I didn't start as a dialect poet. I simply came to the conclusion that I could write it as well, if not better than anybody else I know. And that by doing so I should gain a hearing [for his standard English poetry]. I gained the hearing and now they [the white readers and supporters] don't want me to write anything *but* dialect.

He felt labeled. He was more than a little angry about the turn of events. Paul didn't want to be remembered as a *black* poet, but as a *poet*. There were reasons for his feelings. The times in which he lived helped to shape his and other black people's attitudes—especially the way they saw themselves and the way they wanted others to see them.

Dunbar and the young men and women his age were the first generation of free blacks. They had not been born or raised as slaves, but as free people. Their mothers and fathers had been bound by the physical chains of slavery, but the bold, young turn-of-the-century blacks were fighting to keep from being bound by mental chains that limited their progress and diminished their dreams. It was a battle that they saw themselves losing. And their struggle became more fierce.

Since Frederick Douglass's death, black Americans had not had a spokesman who fearlessly fought in their behalf. And black people were daily losing their rights. Nobody seemed to be able to reverse the growing negative attitudes toward blacks. The ugly facts were becoming clearer and clearer. The slaves had been freed, but their children were still seen as second-class citizens—free, but unequal. It made no sense.

Another man was emerging as the leader of the American black citizenry—Booker T. Washington. Paul had met the kindly schoolteacher at the Chicago World's Columbian Exposition when he stopped to talk with Frederick Douglass. When Paul had been in grade school, Mr. Washington had been establishing a school in Tuskegee, Alabama. From a one-room school with a leaky roof, Washington had built the world-famous Tuskegee Institute, which began graduating productive black citizens more than one hundred years ago—and still is today.

Black Americans were making advancement in all areas of life, but there were some people who were determined that this should not be permitted. These people banded together and formed groups like the Ku Klux Klan, an organization that terrorized the black communities or anyone who offered to help former slaves and their children obtain equal rights guaranteed by the Constitution.

In 1895 at the Cotton States Exposition, Booker T. Washington made the statement, "No race can prosper until it learns that there is as much dignity in tilling the field as in writing a poem." Many people, especially the segregationists, took this to mean that blacks should *only* be educated to become laborers, domestic workers, handymen, and to perform jobs whites didn't want.

The controversy surrounding Washington's statement has been discussed and analyzed by scholars for years. Washington was not the fiery speaker Douglass had been. He chose instead moderation. He stressed making the best of things, avoiding a confrontation between the races at all costs. Some agreed with his theory, but other young black voices rose up in protest. One such voice was W.E.B. DuBois, a young Harvard graduate who opposed Washington. DuBois argued that black people should never compromise their rights as free citizens, even if it meant fighting in court. Later DuBois was to become a founder of the National Association for the Advancement of Colored People (NAACP).

In New York, where Paul was living during this time, young black scholars and men of letters held heated debates about Washington's position. Paul remained, for the most part, silent. He listened in order to learn.

Washington's compromise position had a tremendous impact on Paul's poetry. As a result, educated blacks criticized Paul's poems as playing into the hands of racists. They accused the poet of further compromising the race by representing blacks as being inferior. It was not the poet's representation of his people that was at fault. Rather, it was other people's interpretation of his poems. Dunbar's poems were enjoyed by racists for all the wrong reasons. They used the poet's work to stereotype blacks and to promote their ideas that blacks were ignorant-talking, uneducated people. This is not what Paul wanted to happen. He resented his poems being used that way. This conflict would not be resolved during Dunbar's lifetime.

In spite of his growing concern about the interpretation of his work, Dunbar's poetry brought him fame and a comfortable living. His popularity spread to Europe, and Major Pond decided that Paul should go to England for a tour. Major Pond's daughter, Edith Pond, was leaving in February of 1898 for a trip abroad. Edith was assigned the task of managing Paul's tour.

Plans for his departure began. After a visit to Chicago to say good-bye to Ma, and a stop on the way back to say farewell to Dr. Tobey and Mr. Thatcher, Paul returned to New York. A good friend of his, Mrs. Victoria Earle Matthews, planned a grand send-off party in Paul's honor. The party was the social event of the year among New York blacks. All of Paul's friends were there.

At one point Mrs. Matthews drew Paul aside. She whispered in his ear, "Alice is here." Paul didn't know whether to stand still or run and hide. Before he could decide, he saw her coming toward him. With the light behind her, she looked like a shimmerimg, floating illusion. Was he dreaming? He blinked his eyes. She was standing there. They stood looking into each other's eyes for a moment. She was so pretty—so tiny. Yes, she was real—his Alice.

"I ran away," she said. "I couldn't help it."

For some time now Paul had been wearing Ma's gold wedding ring on his little finger. Later that evening he removed the ring from his finger and placed it on Alice's. "Will you wait for me?" he asked.

"Yes," she answered.

The next morning Paul was at sea aboard the SS *Umbria*. He wrote Ma and told her about the engagement, and then he wrote to Alice—letter after letter after letter.

Paul's trip to England was a success. For several months he was the toast of British society. Still, the trip was not as glamorous as the folks back home might have thought. Paul had suspected that the Ponds were not trustworthy, and his suspicions proved to be well founded.

Miss Pond put him up in a grubby little room in a run-down part of London. He was given very little money. Miss Pond was managing the financial end of the tour, and she claimed all kinds of expenses which were deducted from Paul's share of the profits. In spite of all the highs and lows of the trip, Paul managed to write *The Uncalled*, his first novel.

At last Paul's novelty wore off, and the invitations did too. Miss Pond, using the slimmest of excuses, returned to the United States, leaving Paul stranded in Europe with no money, no work, and no place to stay. He wired Dr. Tobey, who sent return fare immediately.

Once in New York, Paul resumed his writing, first completing "A Negro's Impression of England," while his memories were still fresh. Dodd, Mead accepted *The Uncalled* and issued him a sizeable advance against royalties. He used the money to repay Dr. Tobey for the fare from London and also sent Ma money to return to Dayton. Paul knew that she loved Rob and her grandchildren, but that she longed for the peace and quiet of her little house on Ziegler Street.

Paul was invited to Washington, D.C., by Dr. Kelly Miller, president of Howard University. He accepted the invitation. Will Cook, who wanted desperately to finish *Clorindy*, met him there. Paul had agreed months earlier to help his friend, and now seemed as good a time as any. Will, his brother John, and Paul worked on the musical for hours in the Miller home. The brothers sat at the piano composing music for Paul's lyrics—each one more delightful than the last. At last *Clorindy* was finished; Will and John hurried back to New York to put the work into production.

Then quite unexpectedly, Paul got the stabilizer that he needed to finally marry Alice. A friend helped him secure a job at the Library of Congress starting at $750 a year. Without a moment's delay, he went to Dayton to sell the house on Ziegler Street.

He had expected the move to be quiet and uneventful, but Dayton citizens had other ideas. Paul's high-school classmates gave him a reception, and Captain Stivers, the retired principal of Central High, gave him a handmade violin. Mrs. Conover also entertained Paul in her home.

"Why all the fuss?" he asked Ma shyly. She reminded him that he was Paul Laurence Dunbar now—his name had come to mean something. Still he didn't feel famous. That night Paul wrote to his best friend Bud Burns who was in medical school: "There are a heap of memories clustered around this rickety old house. . . . I missed you. . . ." Paul would miss Dayton, but it was time for him to move on—and up.

Chapter 11

A SEASON OF SORROWS

"Paul Laurence Dunbar, I have a telegram for you." The telegram was from Alice. It contained one word, "Come."

Paul had gone to Washington ahead of Ma. Alice was still teaching, now in Brooklyn, but she and Paul planned to marry in June. Several months earlier Paul had sent her a telegram with one word in it, "Soon." He was making plans for them.

In Washington Paul had found a house big enough for a family. It had a parlor, cherry inlaid wood, and a study with bookcases. It was located in a respectable neighborhood, and the rent was very reasonable—only twenty dollars a month. Everything had moved according to plan. He had a steady job. Ma had arrived. All he needed was Alice.

Alice's parents still opposed her marriage, but she didn't care. There was no reason to wait any longer. Paul agreed. When her telegram arrived, he left for New York.

On the morning of March 6, 1898, Paul Dunbar and Alice Moore were married in the home of Bishop W.B. Derrick. By the first weekend in April, Alice had resigned her teaching post and had moved to Washington as Mrs. Paul Laurence Dunbar.

Alice and Ma got along fine. It was no secret that Ma had a few doubts about her daughter-in-law at first—because of her education. She thought that Alice might feel superior. But Alice proved to be a loving person with a pleasant personality. Besides, she loved Paul. Anybody who loved her son, Ma loved too.

During this period of his life, Paul was as happy as he would ever be; and his work flourished. *Clorindy* opened at the Casino Roof Garden in New York that summer. The show was an instant hit, and so, according to written accounts, were the fashionable Dunbars. They were a very attractive couple.

The Uncalled was published in the fall of 1898. When the author's copies arrived, Alice was surprised to see that the book was dedicated to "my wife." The book received mixed reviews, but still sold very well.

Meanwhile, Paul developed a deep cough. The doctors felt that the dusty volumes at the library were responsible. Alice tried to convince him to quit his job and devote all of his time to writing and giving readings.

Quite by accident Alice helped to make this possible by becoming Paul's business manager. A Western Union messenger delivered a telegram requesting Paul as a speaker. Alice responded to the message, "Will come." Then she wrote, "Fee one hundred dollars." Most speakers of that day were receiving five to fifty dollars for such engagements.

Alice raised the rate, and it was never questioned. Her husband was getting top dollars for his readings. He earned a week's salary in one evening. "Why do you need to work in the library?" she asked.

It was difficult to leave the security of a regular job, but in the end, Alice won. Paul quit his job and became a full-time writer, interrupting his work only to do readings.

Lyrics by the Hearthside was released in February 1899 by Dodd, Mead and Company. Two months later, in April, Paul Dunbar was near death. He had caught a cold while fishing in March with his father-in-law in upstate New York. He had not rested properly and had gone on working. While preparing for a reading, he collapsed and had to be put to bed. Paul was flat on his back at his friend Mrs. Matthews' house in New York. Alice nursed him back to health day by day. Ma wanted to be there too, but Alice convinced Ma that she could take care of her husband.

Afterwards the doctors told Alice that Paul's lungs were in poor condition. To live he would have to have complete bed rest and live in the proper climate. He was told to go to the Catskills in New York and then on to Colorado when he was strong enough to travel.

While Paul was in the Catskills, Dr. Bud Burns, his life-long friend, who was at last a doctor, came to see him and also to serve as his doctor.

The pain in his chest was almost unbearable. To ease the

pain he began to drink—small shots of bourbon at first, then more—and more. Alcohol changed Paul's personality. He would explode if slightly disturbed. But then he could be loving and humorous at other times.

Someone told Paul that a cure for lung disorders was to eat a raw onion every day. So, at bedtime, Paul ate a raw onion and washed it down with beer. Beer and onions!

After six months in high country he was well enough to travel. The Dunbars moved in mid-October to a little town just outside Denver, Colorado. While there, Paul wrote *The Love of Landry*, a light romantic novel, set in the West. It really wasn't a very good book. Some literary historians believe that Paul was trying to prove that a black man could write about something other than blackness. If so, he was right, of course, but failed to realize that writers can write about anything only if they know the subject well. Paul didn't know about the West, cowboy life, or the characters he wrote about. His characters were stiff and their dialog was unreal.

But the writer wasn't worried about public opinion or the principles of good writing at that time. He was getting over a terrible bout with a disease that was slowly draining his life's energy, and he seemed, at that time, just to be happy he was alive. He wrote to friends that he enjoyed writing the novel and the people he met while writing it.

The book was dedicated to Major William Cooke Daniels,

a wealthy man, who liked young Dunbar and had helped him to write the novel with some measure of western authenticity.

The Denver skies were perfect. Sunsets were Paul's favorites. Ma liked to joke with him about never being awake in time to appreciate sunrises. "Never could get that boy up in the morning," Ma told Alice.

Paul laughed, but his poet's mind went to work. Before the week was over, he sat Ma and Alice down to hear his newest poem. "Ma, you'll like this one," he said winking his eye. "It's called 'In the Morning.' "

> *'Lias! 'Lias! Bless de Lawd!*
> *Don' you know de day's erbroad?*
> *Ef you don' git up, you scamp,*
> *Dey 'll be trouble in dis camp.*
> *T'ink I gwine to let you sleep*
> *W'ile I meks yo' boa'd an' keep?*
> *Dat's a putty howdy-do—*
> *Don' you hyeah me, 'Lias—you?*

By the time Paul finished reading the entire poem, Ma was laughing so hard she had tears in her eyes. Alice missed a lot of the humor, because she had not experienced that kind of life. Alice sometimes felt a little left out when Paul and Ma shared some of their early times together. She couldn't help but feel a little jealous.

In May of 1899 the Dunbars went back East. Paul enjoyed visiting with family in Chicago and with Dr. Tobey and old friends in Washington. Alice and Ma stayed in Chicago while Paul went on a speaking tour.

While in Washington the poet had an unusual experience. One evening an elderly gentleman visited the home where Paul was staying. He said he had a story to tell and the poet wondered what the tale would be about: a party, a dinner, a celebration? What? He was in for a real shock.

The old man's voice was hardly a whisper. There was a look in his eyes that might have been terror, or then again, hatred. Paul couldn't tell. But he was certain that he would never forget the old man's eyes as he told his strange tale:

It was his own sister's son who had been taken by the night riders. They came after him because he was supposed to have harmed a white girl. He hadn't, but no one believed him. They strung him to a limb of a giant oak tree. Then they rode off and left his dead body. When his kin had come to cut down his body, every leaf on that tree had withered and dropped off! Not a leaf ever grew again. The oak was haunted.

A cold chill sent shivers through Paul's body. He couldn't wait to get back to his room to start writing. He wrote until his fingers were cramped. The finished poem records the tale of "The Haunted Oak."

The poet starts by asking the tree a question:

110

Pray why are you so bare, so bare,
    Oh, bough of the old oak-tree;
And why, when I go through the shade you throw,
    Runs a shudder over me?

The oak answers:

My leaves were green as the best, I trow,
    And sap ran free in my veins,
But I saw in the moonlight dim and weird
    A guiltless victim's pains.

. . . .

I feel the rope against my bark,
    And the weight of him in my grain,
I feel in the throe of his final woe
    The touch of my own last pain.

Finally the oak says that it is haunted by the spirit of the victim's innocent blood.

Such stories were not uncommon during that time. Racial beatings and lynchings were increasing, and not only in the rural South. Illinois, Ohio, and Indiana also had periods of racial strife.

When "The Haunted Oak" was published, Dunbar's critics cried out that he should stick to dialect.

The fever of racial prejudice was rising higher and higher. Paul lashed out angrily. He wrote a brilliant response to an article written by Charles D. Warner, who suggested that Negroes were not worth trying to educate. New York and Boston were hotbeds of anger on the verge of exploding. It was just a matter of time.

Paul kissed Alice good-bye and set out to do a reading in New York. While he was there, a race riot began. Hundreds were hurt; property damage totaled in the hundreds of thousands of dollars. Paul was caught in the middle of the chaos, but he managed to get to Washington.

Alice met him there. They rented small quarters at 321 Spruce Street, but there wasn't enough room for Ma to come, so she had to stay in Chicago.

Meanwhile, Paul's health was much worse than anybody knew. He was coughing up blood and trying to hide it from Alice. Somehow he managed to smile, even though the pain in his chest was agonizing. Alice had some idea of what her husband was suffering, but he always managed to make a joke to take her mind off his illness.

In order to stay on his feet, he drank, and before long he was drinking too much. Once while very drunk, he gave a reading and embarrassed his host, his family, and himself. Ma forgave Paul without question. She knew something had to be terribly wrong for him to do such a thing. His friends possibly didn't understand, but they forgave him, too. Bud needed no explanation. He knew Paul's condition and offered to help. All those who mattered gave their support—all except Alice. She felt humiliated and embarrassed. Public acceptance was important to her, and Paul had lost a great deal of acceptance. She forgave him, but she never forgot it. Neither did he. Some people believe that this was the beginning of the Dunbars' marital problems.

The nineteenth century ended and the twentieth century began. Paul and Alice quietly celebrated the start of 1900 in their Washington apartment.

Over the next two years Paul wrote another novel, *Sport of the Gods*, and three more books of poetry. He rode as an honored guest in President McKinley's inauguration parade in 1901. Then on September 6, 1901, McKinley was tragically shot and Theodore Roosevelt became the new president of the United States. Roosevelt and Paul met on several occasions, and each time the president proudly acknowledged that he read Dunbar's works with regularity.

Paul Dunbar was sick and getting sicker day by day. He was sensitive and in pain and the coughing spells came more and more frequently. He and Alice began to quarrel.

Although Paul was suffering, he hurt more to see what was happening to his people. Now blacks were not allowed to vote in many states and race riots were exploding all over the country, further separating the races. Schools were being segregated, and the sharecropping system was just as evil as slavery.

Paul saw all this happening to his people. At the same

time, his health was failing rapidly, his marriage was breaking up—his very life was falling apart. His poem, "Sympathy," reveals the inner struggles in the poet's life.

I know what the caged bird feels, alas!
> *When the sun is bright on the upland slopes;*
When the wind stirs soft through the springing grass,
And the river flows like a stream of glass;
> *When the first bird sings and the first bud opes;*
And the faint perfume from its chalice steals—
I know what the caged bird feels!

I know why the caged bird beats his wing
> *Till its blood is red on the cruel bars;*
For he must fly back to his perch and cling
When he fain would be on the bough a-swing;
> *And a pain still throbs in the old, old scars*
And they pulse again with a keener sting—
I know why he beats his wing!

I know why the caged bird sings, ah me,
> *When his wing is bruised and his bosom sore,—*
When he beats his bars and would be free;
It is not a carol of joy or glee,
> *But a prayer that he sends from his heart's deep core,*
But a plea, that upward to Heaven he flings—
I know why the caged bird sings!

Chapter 12

LAY ME DOWN BENEAF DE WILLERS. . .

"We are sorry to inform you that the concert we had planned has been cancelled due to lack of interest. . . ."

This letter was typical of letters Paul had been receiving since word had gotten around that he had a drinking problem. Although he had stopped drinking, people wanted to believe the worst and keep the "Dunbar scandal" alive. Paul said to Ma, "I wish people would mind their own business."

Ma understood, from past experience, how gossip could be hurtful, but she told him that he was a public figure and that everything he did—good or bad—interested people. "That's the price you pay for being famous," she told him.

And the gossips had plenty to chatter about. The Dunbar marriage was crumbling. In January 1902, after a particularly bad argument, Paul walked out on Alice. After a cooling-off period, he was sorry, and tried for a reconciliation. He hadn't stopped loving her. But Alice wouldn't see him or answer his letters, telegrams, or messages. If her intentions were to make him suffer, she succeeded. Those who knew Dunbar best later wrote that he was hurt beyond belief. The battle he was fighting against "those devils in my lungs" was nowhere near as tough as losing "my Alice."

When his health became so poor that it was impossible for

him to work any longer, Paul decided to go home—to die. In October 1903, Paul moved back to Dayton with Ma. His old classmate, Ezra Kuhns, showed him a house on Summit Street. At first glance, Paul knew that the roomy brick house with a barn and grape arbor was his and Ma's home. He could see himself sitting on the porch with the snowball bushes blooming nearby. With the help of friends and family, Paul and Ma moved in. Ma bought hens and planted a city garden—a row of bunch beans, a row of tomatoes, a row of cabbage, and a row of collard greens.

Dr. Bud Burns came to see Paul every day. They played checkers, talked about the time they had been lamplighters, and recalled the play they had given. Paul asked Bud to "Look after Ma. . . when I'm gone." Bud had agreed. He knew that Paul was in pain most of the time; Paul was in the latter stages of tuberculosis. Ma knew, too, that it was just a matter of time. Death was in the Dunbar house and he wasn't leaving until someone went with him.

Bud kept within him a secret he had sworn not to tell. He must have been tempted, many times, to tell his friend, especially knowing how Paul still felt about Alice. Alice had written to Bud asking him to let her know if Paul became very ill. She would come to him. Bud had promised that he would. She had also made the doctor promise that he would not tell Paul about their agreement.

Hardly a day passed that Paul didn't think about Alice—

his last poems reveal it. For a long while he talked about her, but in time he stopped. Her name was rarely mentioned.

Paul Dunbar passed the last days of his life writing, when he could, and entertaining friends who came from all over the country to visit.

People sent him letters and books, flowers, and cookies. One admirer gave him a collie puppy. At that time Paul was nursing a little chick whose mother had been killed. The chick, whose name was Blackie, was trained to follow Paul around like a dog. When the frisky puppy came, Blackie felt safer riding on Paul's shoulder. The pup and the chicken became Paul's constant companions. With a wiggly puppy at his heels and a chicken perched on his shoulder, he was quite a sight. The neighbors had plenty to chatter about. "Honey, you know—they say he drinks a bit," they whispered.

A few people who visited the poet expected to find him somber and solemn, but they were in for a surprise. On one occasion two very proper ladies came to see Paul. They were so stiff and formal he couldn't stand it. He excused himself and returned with Blackie riding on his shoulder. The ladies tried not to look at the chicken on their host's shoulder. If he didn't mention it, they certainly weren't going to. But, Blackie was making such a fuss that one of the ladies finally asked very icily, "Mr. Dunbar, is that a chicken?"

"No, madam," he answered as straight-faced as he could, "it is a pig."

At first the women were stunned. Then they saw Paul's black marble face relax into a smile. They couldn't help but smile, too. Once the ice was broken, Paul had his visitors laughing. It was a memorable afternoon for them all.

Letters continued to pour in daily. One letter particularly touched the poet. "I'll never again be ashamed I'm black." If his poems had done that, then he knew he had not written without purpose.

On June 27, 1904, when Paul was thirty-three years old, his friends gave him a wonderful surprise birthday party. It was like a reunion with Charley Higgins, Randy Tamms, and Bud there to help him celebrate.

Then one day in the fall of that same year, Bud didn't come. All day Paul fretted about where his friend might be. Then he finally learned the awful truth: Bud was dead. He had died suddenly, without warning.

Paul insisted that he go to the cemetery, although it was cold and damp. He stood at the grave site until he had to be forced to leave. He never accepted Bud's death. He was prepared for his own death, but not Bud's. Who would care for Ma? He had so depended on his childhood friend.

On a cold February day in 1905, Paul Laurence Dunbar died. The neighbors on Summit Street noted that the Dunbars had a black wreath on their door. They knew that Paul had died, and according to tradition, they sent over cakes, pies, a pot of greens, candied yams—anything to help. They visited too, but the real visiting would come later when Matilda needed someone—in the spring when the snowball trees bloomed and Paul wouldn't be there to enjoy them.

Matilda Dunbar grieved, but she carried out her son's last wishes. In a poem he had written long ago he had said:

> *Lay me down beneaf de willers in de grass,*
> *Whah de branch 'll go a-singin' as it pass.*
>   *An' w'en I 's a-layin' low,*
>   *I kin hyeah it as it go*
> *Singin', "Sleep, my honey, tek yo' res' at las'."*

His funeral services were short and simple, and Ma planted a willow tree beside his grave.

When Alice read about her husband's death, she was hurt and a bit confused. Bud had promised that he would get in touch with her when Paul was very ill. She wrote to Bud, and somehow the letter finally came to Ma. Reading it, she could only wonder why Alice had not come to see Paul earlier. Ma was not one to be bitter, but she was never able to truly understand what had happened between Alice and her son.

Ma didn't change a thing in Paul's room; it stayed as it was. Even the last thing he was writing was left on the desk—a poem dedicated to Bud. Up until her death, Ma dusted the room and kept it looking as though the poet had just stepped out and would return momentarily.

Alice became a writer of some note. When, in time, she remarried, she kept Dunbar as part of her name. It is from her biography of Paul that we know a great deal about him.

At the time of his death, the *Boston Transcript* said this about the young writer from Dayton:

> The death of Paul Laurence Dunbar is a loss to American letters. He was not, perhaps, a great poet, but he was a real one. . . . He won a place in American literature of which he cannot be deprived by prejudice, because its history would be incomplete without the fine elements which he supplied.

Today Paul Dunbar is one of our national treasures. Nikki Giovanni, a twentieth-century American poet, had this to say about him:

> Dunbar preserved a part of our history. And accurately. It would be foolish to say all blacks struggled against slavery as it would to say all acquiesced to it. The truth lies somewhere in the blending. Perhaps Dunbar's greatest triumph is that he has survived all those who would use his gift for their own dead-end purposes.

Paul Laurence Dunbar was different from the other poets

of his day. He took a chance. People have debated the pros and cons of his writing ever since "A Banjo Song" was first published. Yet, for generations young readers have been discovering "Little Brown Baby," "An Ante-Bellum Sermon," and "The Party." They don't seem to care about what the critics have to say. Dunbar took a chance when he wrote in slave dialect, but the world is richer because he did.

Paul Laurence Dunbar 1872-1906

1872 Paul Laurence Dunbar is born.

1874 Disraeli becomes prime minister of Britain for second time. The elephant is made a symbol of the Republican party when Thomas Nast uses it in a cartoon in *Harper's Weekly*.

1875 Congress passes Civil Rights Act giving Negroes some of the same rights as whites.

1876 Battle of Little Bighorn; General Custer defeated by Sioux and Cheyenne. Alexander Graham Bell patents telephone. Mark Twain publishes *The Adventures of Tom Sawyer*.

1877 Reconstruction in the South ends. Rebellion in Japan put down. Porfirio Diaz becomes president of Mexico, remains in power until 1911.

1878 Albert A. Michelson, German-American scientist, accurately measures speed of light at 186,508 miles per second. Thomas Edison patents the phonograph.

1879 Edison invents the first practical electric light. George Selden, an American, invents an internal combustion engine that can be used in a "horseless carriage."

1880 Supreme Court rules that it is unconstitutional to prevent Negroes from being on juries. Joel Chandler Harris publishes *Uncle Remus: His Songs and His Sayings*. Mark Twain publishes *A Tramp Abroad*.

1881 President Garfield is assassinated in Washington, D.C. Alexander II of Russia is assassinated. Booker T. Washington becomes president of the Normal and Industrial Institute for Negroes (later to be called Tuskegee Institute). Louis Pasteur, a Frenchman, vaccinates sheep against anthrax.

1883 Discovery by Edison that electric current can be sent through space. Twain publishes *Life on the Mississippi*. Programs of social reform begun in Germany. Supreme Court declares Civil Rights Act of 1875 unconstitutional, except for the section dealing with jury duty.

1884 In the South, Ku Klux Klan stops Negroes from voting; Supreme Court rules that this is a federal offense. Twain publishes *The Adventures of Huckleberry Finn*.

1885 Apaches leave their reservation and start war with whites. Pasteur develops rabies vaccine.

1886 The Statue of Liberty is dedicated in New York Harbor. War with Apaches ends with Chief Geronimo's surrender. Haymarket Square riot occurs in Chicago after protest over treatment of workers in a labor strike; police try to squelch protest.

1887 U.S. obtains right to build naval base at Pearl Harbor in Hawaii. Queen Victoria of England celebrates Golden Jubilee. French form Indo-China.

1889 Several states pass first antitrust laws. First whites settle in Oklahoma. Frederick Douglass is appointed minister-resident and consul-general to the Republic of Haiti.

1890 Sherman Antitrust Act passed. Battle of Wounded Knee; Sioux massacred. Dunbar publishes the *Tattler*, a black newspaper. Japan holds its first general election.

1891 Indian territory once belonging to the Sauk, Fox, and Pottawatomi opened to settlement by whites.

1892 Harris publishes *Nights with Uncle Remus*. Prime Minister Gladstone of Britain attempts to get home rule for Ireland. Famine in Russia. Nationalist movement in India gains momentum.

1893 Economic depression begins in U.S. Hawaii claimed as U.S. protectorate. World's Columbian Exposition held in Chicago; Frederick Douglass is appointed Haitian commissioner at the exposition. Dunbar publishes *Oak and Ivy*. Wright brothers open a shop to manufacture, repair, and sell bicycles.

1894 Pullman Company strike in Chicago led by Eugene V. Debs, who is jailed. Hawaiian Republic receives U.S. recognition. *Century* magazine publishes three of Dunbar's poems. French army officer Alfred Dreyfus falsely convicted of treason. Last tsar of Russia, Nicholas II, takes the throne. Korea and Japan declare war on China.

1895 Cubans revolt against Spanish rule. An Italian, Guglielmo Marconi, invents wireless telegraph. Treaty of Shimonoseki ends Chinese-Japanese War. Death of Frederick Douglass.

1896 Dunbar's second book of poems, *Majors and Minors*, is published. *Plessy v. Ferguson* Supreme Court decision makes "separate but equal" accommodations for blacks and whites legal. Dunbar publishes *Lyrics of Lowly Life*. French scientist Henri Becquerel discovers radioactivity.

1898 Dunbar marries Alice Ruth Moore. *Clorindy*, a musical play for which Dunbar wrote the lyrics, opens in New York. Dunbar's first novel, *The Uncalled*, is published. Spanish-American War; Treaty of Paris ending war results in the U.S. receiving Puerto Rico, Guam, and the Philippines. Cuba gains independence. Beginning of German naval expansion. Social Democratic party established in Russia.

1899 Filipinos revolt against Americans; Wake Island annexed by U.S. Beginning of Boer War in South Africa between Boers and British.

1900 Hawaii becomes U.S. territory. Civil government set up for Puerto Rico. Danish scientist Niels Bohr proposes theory of how the atom is structured, which is still valid today.

1901 President McKinley is assassinated by an anarchist. Cuba becomes a U.S. protectorate. In Britain, Queen Victoria dies; Edward VII becomes king. In Russia, Social Revolutionary party is founded, calling for a revolution.

1902 Congress approves money to build the Panama Canal. Treaty of Vereeniging ends Boer War.

1903 Treaty between the U.S. and Panama gives the U.S. the land across which the Panama Canal will be built. The Menshevik and Bolshevik factions of the Russian Social Democratic party are born; the two become separate parties. Orville and Wilbur Wright make the world's first successful airplane flights.

1904 Harris publishes *The Tar Baby*. Russian-Japanese war begins.

1905 Nicholas II of Russia signs the October Manifesto promising government reforms that will give more freedom to his subjects. Albert Einstein, German scientist, proposes his theory of relativity. Russian-Japanese War ended by Treaty of Portsmouth. Revolutionary league established in China by Sun-Yat-sen; its goal is to overthrow the Manchu dynasty.

1906 Paul Laurence Dunbar dies. Anti-Negro riot in Atlanta. Massive earthquake in San Francisco destroys a large section of the city. First Duma (representative legislature) meets in Russia. Dreyfus is cleared of the charge of treason and is awarded the Legion of Honor.

Africa, 22

A.M.E. Methodist Church, 28, 29

"Ante-Bellum Sermon, An" (poem), 91, 121

Back to Africa Movement, 22

"Banjo Song, A" (poem), 47-50, 121

Baptist Church, Yellow Springs, Ohio, 35

Becca, Aunt (great-grandmother), 19, 20

Beecher, Henry Ward, 94

"blackface" (minstrel show), 32-34

black poet laureate, 49

Blocher (printer), 54-56

"Boogie Man," 51

Boston, Massachusetts, 95, 112

Boston Transcript (newspaper), 120

Burns, Robert ("Bud"), 20, 21, 23, 24, 26, 27, 30, 32, 40, 78, 103, 107, 112, 116, 118, 119

Butler, Reverend, 28

Cable, George, 79

Calahan Building, 41, 42, 44, 45, 54, 60, 77, 84

Canada, 14

Carrothers, James, 72

Casino Roof Garden, New York, 106

Catskills, New York, 107

Central High School, 30-32, 35, 38, 103

Century (magazine), 42, 78, 79

Chapman, Dr. W.C., 57-59, 74

Chicago, Illinois, 44, 60, 70, 72-75, 77, 86, 87, 95, 98, 101, 110, 112

Chicago News Record (newspaper), 47

Civil War, 12, 14, 40, 73

Cleveland, Ohio, 78

Clorindy, the Origin of the Cakewalk (musical), **68**, 87, 103, 106

Colorado, 107, 108

Colored Americans' Day, 74

Conover, Mrs. Frank, 42, 54, 56, 57, 79, 84, 85, 103

Cook, John, 103

Cook, Will, 86, 103

Cotton States Exposition, 99

"Crisis, The" (poem), 93

Daniels, Major William Cooke, 108

"Dawn" (poem), 93

Dayton, Ohio, 9, 12, 19, 20, 22, 24, 25, 32, 35, 56, 59, **64**, 77, 79, 80, 83, 88, 93, 94, 102, 103, 104, 116

"Dayton at the Fair" (article), 60

Dayton Herald (newspaper), 31, 35, 37-40, 42, 60

Deac (nickname), 27

Denver, Colorado, 108, 109

Derrick, Bishop W.B., 105

Detroit, Michigan, 57

dialect poems, 47-51, 74, 88, 91, 96, 97, 121

Dodd, Mead and Company (publisher), 95, 96, 102, 107

Douglass, Frederick, 40, **65**, 70, 72-76, 77, 90, 94, 98, 99

Douglass, Joseph, 70, 72, 73

DuBois, W.E.B., 99, 100

Dunbar, Alice Ruth Moore (wife), **67**, 79, 80, 86-88, 90, 95, 101, 103, 105-110, 112, 113, 115, 116, 119, 120

Dunbar, Elizabeth (sister), 14

Dunbar, Joshua ("Pa") (father), 10, 11, 13-16, 18, 21-23, 51

Dunbar, Matilda ("Ma") (mother), 9-31, 34-41, 45-49, 55, 56, 60, **62**, 74, 75, 77-80, 83, 85, 87, 89, 93, 95, 96, 101-103, 105-107, 109, 110, 112, 115, 116, 118, 119

Dunbar, Paul Laurence: birth, 9-11; family background, 12-14, 19-22; parents' divorce, 15, 16; early schooling, 17-20; first poem, 19; mother's stories, 20-22; death of father, 23; lamplighter job, 23-25; at Intermediate School, 26, 27; first poetry recitation, 28, 29; at high school, 30-32, 38; at minstrel show, 32-34; drama club, 34, 35; first printed poem, 35, 36; job hunting, 37-41; and racial bigotry, 37-40, 98-100; as elevator operator, 41, 42, 45, 77, 84; "Ode to Ethiopia" poem, 42-44, 58, 59; as story writer, 44; poetry recitals,

45, 56-59; dialect poems, 47-51, 88, 96, 97; "Little Brown Baby" poem, 51-53; first book of poetry, 54-56; at Chicago exposition, 60, 70, 72-75; and Frederick Douglass, 72-76; poems in *Century*, 78, 79; romance with Alice Moore, 79, 80, 86, 95, 101; "The Party" poem, 80-83; and Dr. H.A. Tobey, 84-88, 93, 102; second book of poetry, 88-93; in New York City, 94, 95, 100; third book of poetry, 96, 97; England tour, 100-102; job at Library of Congress, 103; marriage, 105; Alice as business manager, 106, 107; illness, 107, 108, 112-116; drinking, 108, 112, 115; in Colorado, 108, 109; "The Haunted Oak" poem, 110, 111; marital problems, 113-115; last days, 117, 118; death, 118-120
Dunbar, Paul Laurence, (illustrations): 2, **8, 66**
"Easter Ode, An" (poem), 28, 29
Elizabeth (aunt), 49
Emancipation Proclamation, 12, 22
England, 100, 102
Festival Hall, Columbian Exposition, 75
Field, Eugene, 47
Fifth District School, 18, 19
Fifty-Fifth Division, 14
"Frederick Douglass" (poem), 76, 90
Giovanni, Nikki, 120
Glass family, 21
Haiti, 72-74, 77
Hallowell, Colonel Norwood Penrose, 14
Harper Appleton (publisher), 95
Harper's Weekly (magazine), 91, 92
Harris, Joel Chandler, 48, 49
Harvard University, 59, 87, 99
"Haunted Oak, The" (poem), 110, 111
Higgins, Charlie, 26, 27, 30, 32, 40, 77, 118
house, Summit Street, Dayton, Ohio, **69,** 116, 118
Howard Street, Dayton, Ohio, 9, 12, 16, 19, 20
Howard University, 103
Howells, William Dean, 91-93, 96, 97
Indianapolis, Indiana, 79, 80, 83
Intermediate School, 24-27, 30, 31

"In the Morning" (poem), 109
Jim Crow laws, 42
Johnson, James Weldon, 97
Johnson, R.U., 79
"Jump back, honey, jump back," 71, 72, 79
Kellogg Syndicate, 44
Kentucky, 12, 19, 21
Knights of Pythias Hall, 32
Kuhns, Ezra, 26, 30, 31, 116
Ku Klux Klan, 99
Library of Congress, 103
Life and Times (autobiography of F. Douglass), 75
Lincoln, Abraham, 12, 22
"Little Billy" (story), 44
"Little Brown Baby" (poem), 51-53, 121
Liza (grandmother), 19, 20
London, England, 102
Longfellow, Henry Wadsworth, 60
Love of Landry, The (novel), 108
Lowell, James Russell, 47
Lyrics by the Hearthside (book of poetry), 107
Lyrics of Lowly Life (book of poetry), 96
Majors and Minors (book of poetry), 88-91
Matthews, Dr. J.N., 45
Matthews, Victoria Earle, 101, 107
McKinley, William, 113
Midget, The (newspaper), 36, 54
Miller, Dr. Kelly, 103
minstral shows, 32-34, 48
Moore, Alice Ruth (*See* Dunbar, Alice Ruth Moore)
Murphy, Ethel (niece), 89
Murphy, Leckie (Mrs. Robert), 77, 87
Murphy, Robert ("Rob") (half brother), 12, 14, 16-19, 22, 23, 26, 29, 60, 74, 77, 87, 89, 95, 102
Murphy, William ("Will") (half brother), 12, 14, 16-18, 23, 29, 60
Murphy, Willis, 12, 22
National Association for the Advancement of Colored People (NAACP), 100
National Cash Register Company, 41
"Negro in the South, The" (lecture), 57
"Negro Love Song, A" (poem), 71, 72, 79, 86

"Negro's Impression of England, A" (article), 102

New York City, 94, 100-102, 103, 105-107, 112

Oak and Ivy (book of poetry), 54-57, 74, 84, 85, 88

"Ode to Colored Americans" (poem), 75

"Ode to Ethiopia" (poem), 42-44, 55, 58, 59, 74

Ohio River, 14

"Ol' Tunes, The" (poem), 74

"On the River" (poem), 35, 36

"Our Martyred Soldiers" (poem), 35

"Party, The" (poem), 80-83, 121

Philodramians, 34

"plantation talk," 21, 48

Pond, Edith, 100-102

Pond, Major James B., 94, 95, 100, 102

"Race Problem in America, The" (speech), 75

Reeves, Dr., 78

Riley, James Whitcomb, 47, 49, 60

Roosevelt, Theodore, 113

"sittin' out," 9

slave dialect, 21, 47-51, 121

Soldier's Retirement Home, Dayton, 16, 22

Sport of the Gods (novel), 113

Spruce Street, Washington, D.C., 112

State Mental Hospital, 87

"Steal Away" (song), 23, 25

Steele, Samuel, 19, 20

Stivers, Captain (school principal), 30, 32, 37, 103

Stolen Calf, The (play), 34, 35

Stowe, Harriet Beecher, 94

Summit Street, Dayton, Ohio, **69**, 116, 118

"Swing Low, Sweet Chariot" (song), 23

"Sympathy" (poem), 114

Tamms, Randolph ("Randy"), 29, 30, 32, 40, 78, 118

Tattler (newspaper), 38

"Tenderfoot, The" (story), 44

Tenth District School, 20, 25, 26

Thatcher, Charles, 57, 59, 78, 85, 87, 88, 101

Third District School, 20

Tobey, Dr. H.A., 84-88, 91, 93, 94, 101, 102, 110

Toledo, Ohio, 57, 84, 93

Toledo Blade and *Bee* (newspapers), 59

Truesdell, Helen, 44

Tuskegee, Alabama, 98

Tuskegee Institute, 99

Twain, Mark, 94

Umbria, S.S. (ship), 101

Uncalled, The (novel), 102, 106

Uncle Remus stories, 48, 49

Uncle Tom's Cabin, 94

Underground Railroad, 14

Union army, 12

United Brethren Publishing House, 54-55

United States Supreme Court, 41

Warner, Charles D., 112

Washington, Booker T., 98-100

Washington, D.C., 103, 105, 110, 112, 113

Watkins (English teacher), 31

West End Club, Toledo, Ohio, 57, 59

Western Reserve medical school, 78

Western Writers' Association, 45, 84, 86

West Side Lodge #5, 32

"We Wear the Mask" (poem), 91

"When I Get to Heaven" (song), 23

"When Malindy Sings" (poem), 89, 90

Wilson, Professor, 28

Witmark Music Publishers, 86

World (newspaper), 79

World's Columbian Exposition, 60, 70, 72-75, 95, 98

Wright, Orville, 26, 30, 35, 38, 54, 55, **63**, 77

Wright, Wilbur, 26, 35, 38, 54, **63**

Yellow Springs, Ohio, 35

Ziegler Street, Dayton, Ohio, 56, 102, 103

ABOUT THE AUTHOR

Patricia C. McKissack and her husband, Fredrick, are freelance writers, editors, and teachers of writing. They are the owners and operators of All-Writing Services, located in Clayton, Missouri. Ms. McKissack, an award-winning editor, published author, and experienced educator, has taught writing at several St. Louis colleges and universities, including Lindenwood College, the University of Missouri at St. Louis, and Forest Park Community College.

Since 1975, Ms. McKissack has published numerous magazine articles and stories for juvenile and adult readers. She has written another biography in the People of Distinction series, *Martin Luther King, Jr: A Man to Remember*. She has also conducted educational and editorial workshops throughout the country for a number of organizations, businesses, and universities.

Patricia McKissack is the mother of three teenage sons. They all live in a large remodeled inner-city home in St. Louis. Aside from writing, which she considers a hobby as well as a career, Ms. McKissack likes to take care of her many plants.